Fresh W
of the Spirit

Fresh Winds of the Spirit

Liturgical Resources for Year A

Lavon Bayler

The Pilgrim Press
NEW YORK

Library of Congress Cataloging-in-Publication Data

Bayler, Lavon, 1933–
    Fresh winds of the spirit.

    Includes indexes.
    1. Worship programs.   I. Title.
BV198.B29   1986   264   86-21191
ISBN 0-8298-0736-5 (pbk.)

2d printing, 1988

The Pilgrim Press, 132 West 31 Street, New York, New York 10001

*To Elsie Dickel Burrichter,
my first teacher,
with whom I worshiped often
in churches my father served,
and
Ethel Shellenberger,
my adolescent inspiration,
who demonstrated to
national youth caravaners
the centrality of
worship
to the Christian life*

Contents

Foreword

In *Fresh Winds of the Spirit* Lavon Bayler has combined poetic images and rhythms with scriptural allusions and resonances to provide resources that will enrich the life of any congregation that uses them.

A rich variety of resources, including hymn texts, is provided for each set of lectionary readings for Year A. The readings are reflected in prayers and litanies in a creative way that draws the worshiper into appropriating God's grace and accepting the challenges of faithful living. Indeed, these worship texts may well be an opening into the scriptures, as the preacher looks for an organizing theme for the sermon.

Good worship resources are of high aesthetic quality; they resemble poetry more than prose. Vivid imagery embodies concepts that might otherwise be more appropriate for theological treatises than for worship. Rhythmic language unites a congregation in one voice. Words are common and simple enough not to call attention to themselves, yet (as John Calvin insisted) should be of enough weight and dignity to be worthy of their purpose: the praise of God. At the same time, good worship resources have a freshness and honesty of expression that sometimes startles, instead of moving in the same old ruts. Bayler's work displays all these aesthetic qualities.

Planning worship based on the lectionary often makes me aware that there is a need for hymn texts that draw on parts of scripture other than the psalms and that express contemporary theological concerns. Bayler has provided such a hymn text for each Sunday of Year A, which can be sung to hymn tunes known to any congregation. The texts express the faith of the church in fresh ways that are faithful to scripture and Christian tradition.

My first meeting with Lavon Bayler was in 1973. At that time she was pastor of First Congregational Church, Carpentersville, Illinois, and she was calling a group together in the Illinois Conference UCC to work on women's issues in the church. She was personally supportive to me at a time when I was finding little encouragement as a woman seeking to enter the ordained ministry. I bear a personal debt to her, but so do great numbers of women and men in the church, for her efforts for justice have been tireless.

Bayler was a key contributor to my books of worship resources, *Bread for the Journey* and *Flames of the Spirit*. Now, in her own book, she brings us her sensitivity to word and worship and her poetic gifts. Her concerns for justice in the world are reflected week after week not only through consistent use of inclusive language, but also in intercession for the world's people and confession of barriers that keep us from solidarity with them all.

I commend to you this book that, above all, allows the scripture to speak in and through the worship of the church.

Ruth C. Duck

Introduction

As a child, gazing out a window during a storm, I saw a giant maple tree lifted from the ground and toppled into the street. When the wind blows, its awesome power can terrify.

On a warm morning, I ventured forth to greet the dawn and felt a kindly caress on my brow. When the wind blows, its gentle presence can reassure.

God is Wind—Breath—Spirit. When the wind blows, we are moved to worship. Fresh winds of the Spirit brings God's power and gentleness into the sanctuary where we can only bow in awe, and then dare to hear and heed God's latest call to us.

As I studied the scriptures for each occasion of the Church Year (series A), I was refreshed and renewed. All the liturgical elements in this book grew out of my daily encounter with the biblical record. Throughout the experience of writing, I felt the Spirit's presence.

Now it is my prayer that God may breathe new vitality into your life and ministry as you read the Bible passages and all the resources based on them. May your preparation and worship be enriched by *Fresh Winds of the Spirit.*

Recently I completed a most refreshing and rewarding three-month sabbatical leave from my responsibilities as an Area Conference Minister for the United Church of Christ in Illinois. A substantial portion of the time away from my ministry with pastors, congregations, and committees of Northern Association was spent immersed in the scriptures of the Common Texts and COCU* lectionaries for Year A of the three-year cycle. No similar period of my life has been marked by such intensive Bible study; it was a profoundly meaningful spiritual pilgrimage. These liturgical resources and hymns are the results of my reflection and writing. Aware that they do not convey the full power of the biblical revelation, I offer them with the prayer that they may assist you in your journey with the same scriptures.

The idea for this book emerged slowly from several years of preparing similar material for Lent for the clergy of our Association.

*Consultation on Church Union

A number of my colleagues found this assistance helpful in their worship preparations during a busy season of the Church Year and asked for more. Some used the resources in their entirety; others chose, cut, and edited to serve their particular purposes.

As this book has emerged, it has been my hope to make available more material than most services will require. A number of the responsive calls to worship and service endings are designed so the leader's part is coherent without the congregational response, and thus can be used alone. Because these readings often reflect several or all of the suggested biblical references for the day, you may want to edit the responses to emphasize the scripture you have chosen for central interpretation. During some seasons a confessional service is provided, while in others an invocation is substituted. Sometimes, with minor changes, either of these can be adapted to the other format.

Because liturgy is "the work of the people," I encourage extensive participation by the congregation, not just in the words and actions of the worship services, but also in preparation for them. Small groups, discussing the scriptures in light of personal experience and current events some time before the service of worship, give promise of more alert and involved worshipers and more relevant sermons. When such gatherings occur, prayers and readings from this book might be used to enrich the experience. Participants could then be invited to adapt the resources for local use or compose their own liturgies on the basis of the group's meditation and study.

With the emergence of a new book of worship in many denominations, it is hoped that this book will supplement the liturgical materials found there. We need standard worship forms that are repeated again and again, the prayers that become so familiar that their cadences are called to mind in our everyday decision-making and reverie. But most of us also appreciate fresh ways to address God. When the prayers reinforce the message of the day's scripture, there's a better-than-average chance that we will carry their truth into our daily lives.

For congregations that do not follow the lectionary, the indexes—prepared by David Bayler—should be especially helpful. Whether one is starting from a particular scripture passage or with a certain theme in mind, a way is provided to locate quickly some materials that may be incorporated into worship. Smaller gatherings within the community of faith can also benefit when leaders consult the Index of Themes and Key Words or the Index of Scripture Readings.

Some of the resources are useful for devotional times in church organizations and committees.

Both clergy and laity may use this book for their personal devotions. How powerful corporate worship would be if, all during the week, participants had immersed themselves in the scriptures and prayers to be used on Sunday morning! Churches that follow the lectionary will find this book a helpful resource in their hymnal racks. Members may also want personal copies at home. Note the appendix of new hymn texts prepared especially to reinforce the scriptural message for each worship occasion. A Topical Index of Hymns makes these texts useful beyond the particular time for which they were written.

Words are only part of the total worship experience. They are symbols through which we seek to communicate with one another and express ourselves to our Creator. For those accustomed to public speaking and reading aloud, words can be powerful vehicles. But many people will be reached more deeply by music, visual arts, or touch. Every member and visitor needs friendly greetings of other worshipers, the responsive listening and inquiry of concerned church leaders, and frequent opportunities to practice the faith in programs of outreach and service. Significant worship and human interaction require careful planning and preparation.

Appreciation is expressed to colleagues in ministry who took time from their busy schedules to read and comment on portions of the manuscript. Thanks to Doug Anders, Christine Barton, Bob Dell, Evelyn Dickerson, Pat Flynn, Keith Karau, Pat Kitner, Carol Munro, and Dick Nye for their suggestions, some of which are incorporated in the text. I am also grateful to Dave Williams for contributing several of his hymns and to Mary Cathey, director of Christian education for The National Presbyterian Church in Washington, D.C., who took such an interest in the project that she undertook the assignment of writing more than a dozen new hymn texts, as well as donating several she had written earlier. Her involvement came from a "chance" meeting at an ecumenical conference of Christian educators. Special appreciation is due my understanding family, with special thanks for the encouragement of my husband, Bob, and my staff colleague, "Clip" Higgins. Completion of the project would have been virtually impossible without the careful typing of my secretary and friend, Inge Bisanz. For her involvement a simple thank you is woefully inadequate. She was ably assisted in this task by Nancy Sakalauski.

Liturgical Resources
for Year A

The Advent Season

First Sunday of Advent

Old Testament: Isaiah 2:1–5
Psalm 122
Epistle: Romans 13:8–14
Gospel: Matthew 24:36–44

CALL TO WORSHIP

Wake up, people of God!
Our salvation is near!
We have been asleep and did not know it.
Christ comes to awaken all our potential.
God's law of love summons us away
from actions that hurt and destroy.
We seek to know the ways of God
and to walk in the light where Christ leads.
Let us enter this season of preparation,
expecting to be changed as we worship and serve.
We will watch and ready ourselves
for the coming of One whom God sends.

INVOCATION

Great God, whom our spiritual ancestors worshiped on the mountain, lift us up in anticipation of Christ's advent among us. Grant us the vision to see beyond ourselves and to view all humankind as neighbors. Help us to be honest, generous, and merciful in all our relationships. We would attune ourselves to matters of the Spirit so we will be ready for Christ's coming. To that end, bless our worship today, in Jesus' name. Amen.

CALL TO CONFESSION

People of faith recognize a purpose in life that points to God's law. Though far beyond our comprehension, it was summed up by Jesus in the love of neighbor. Human violation of God's intention brings us to our knees in search of a Savior. Let us confess our sin.

PRAYER OF CONFESSION

God of peace, we have lifted up swords against our enemies and violated the trust of our sisters and brothers. We have used people for our own ends and misused the riches of your grace in destructive ways that threaten our well-being and that of others. We are not ready for you to visit us and call us to account. O God, we would cast off the works of night and live anew in the light of your day. Decide for us, not against us, we pray, as we ask your forgiveness and seek to put on Christ, in whose name we pray. Amen.

ASSURANCE OF FORGIVENESS

Our only debt is to love. God lifts the terrible burden of our sin so we can walk in newness of life. Christ goes with us, transforming time, and making us whole. Let us be alert and teachable as we dwell in God's light!

COLLECT (PRAYER OF PREPARATION BEFORE THE SCRIPTURES)

As you draw especially near to us, O God, through these words we call holy, equip us to fulfill your law of love. Move us beyond quarreling, jealousy, and self-centered pursuits that we may come to understand and appreciate those other individuals and other nations with whom we share your planet Earth. Grant that a larger view of who we are and whose we are will move us to beat our swords into plowshares and our spears into pruning hooks. Amen.

OFFERTORY PRAYER

Eternal God, whose gift of love we can never repay, we offer these symbols of our gratitude. May they equip our church to minister more alertly and lovingly in this community and beyond. Amen.

COMMISSION AND BLESSING

Be watchful and compassionate in these days of Advent;
   God meets us in both friend and stranger.
We will be alert to Christ's presence within us
   and in unexpected places and people.
God's love in Christ knows no limits;
   it summons us to extend ourselves in new ways.
We hear Christ's call to love our neighbors
   and do no wrong to them.
God's love in Christ is poured out on every one of us,
   inviting us to appreciate our own worth.
We will walk in the ways of God,
   rejoicing that God cares for us.
Go in peace. Be peacemakers.
   Live fully, in the present moment, as if it were your last. Amen.
Amen.

Second Sunday of Advent

Old Testament: Isaiah 11:1–10
                  Psalm 72:1–8
Epistle: Romans 15:4–13
Gospel: Matthew 3:1–12

CALL TO WORSHIP

Welcome to this service of prayer and praise.
  Rejoice together, people of God.
We anticipate the coming of God's chosen one,
  who brings hope to the meek of the earth.
The promises of God are for all humankind,
  Jew and Gentile, rich and poor, slave and free.
We are called to live in harmony,
  even with those who appear to be enemies.
We shall be judged, not by our connections,
  but by our commitment to God's purposes.
We draw near for instruction and encouragement,
  to be girded with righteousness and faithfulness.

INVOCATION

God, whom we fear and in whom we hope, awaken all our senses to the meaning of Christ's coming. Baptize us with the Holy Spirit and with fire that we may be alert to opportunities for faithful witness and deeds of service. We would welcome one another in this service of worship as Christ has welcomed us. Grant us your joy and peace as we learn and serve together. Amen.

CALL TO CONFESSION

Out of the myriad cries of this season comes one that few hear and even fewer heed: "Repent, for God's realm is at hand." In moments of silence, ponder which of these written petitions applies to you. Then let each of us pray those parts of the prayer that we can utter in sincere penitence.

PRAYER OF CONFESSION

Awesome God, whom we have ignored amid the world's pretensions, we confess that we have been impressed by appearances and power. We divide people into classes and categories and choose to associate with those who seem most likely to benefit us. Accumulation of things has been more important to us than wisdom and understanding. We are more attracted to might than to good counsel. We seldom ponder equity for the poor or work on ways to accomplish the revolution of true peace in the world. Forgive, O God, our failure to see and hear your revelation. We repent and seek a new way. Amen.

ASSURANCE OF FORGIVENESS

We cannot presume on God's favor because we have been faithfully religious. But honest sorrow over the way we have treated others and failed to live up to God's purposes is met with understanding, forgiveness, and the opportunity to make a new start. Let all people praise God and bear fruit that benefits repentance.

COLLECT

Reveal yourself anew, God of all creation, in ways that we can understand. Turn us around so we may join the meek of the earth in welcoming your advent. We long for that day of peace when all your people bear good fruit and childlike trust leads us all in the way of peace. Amen.

OFFERTORY PRAYER

With these offerings we move beyond words to deeds, O God. We share good news and seek the peace you alone can give. We express our faith in your goodness and in the witness our church can make in a needy world. May these gifts be wheat and not chaff in the realm of heaven. Amen.

COMMISSION AND BLESSING

May the God of hope fill you
 with all joy and peace in believing.
How good it is to visit God's holy mountain,
 to have this time apart from our busy world.
By the power of the Holy Spirit
 may you abound in hope.
How good it is to return to our busy world,
 filled with new expectation
 and renewed capacity to share.
May the One whom the nations seek
 visit you in your home and work and leisure.
May we bear good fruit among all people
 and live in harmony with our sisters and brothers.
Amen. **Amen.**

Third Sunday of Advent

Old Testament: Isaiah 35:1–10
 Psalm 146:5–10
Epistle: James 5:7–10
Gospel: Matthew 11:2–11

CALL TO WORSHIP

Rejoice with great joy and singing,
>   for you shall see the glory of God.
How shall we see the Sovereign One,
>   **and where is joy to be found?**
God has promised to come to us,
>   with saving grace to meet our need.
We are weighed down with limitations
>   **and oppressed by many fears.**
God breaks into the deserts of our despair
>   with springs of water to quench our thirst.
Grant us strength and patience
>   **to await God's coming and receive the good news.**

INVOCATION

Open our eyes and unstop our ears lest we miss your surprises, O God. Heal our arthritic spirits, which have been more disabling than weak hands and feeble knees. May we find in this hour of worship good reason for everlasting joy and gladness. Amen.

CALL TO CONFESSION

God calls us, grumblers and spiritual cripples, to examine ourselves. The world that, in our sinful state, seems like a barren desert may hold more beauty than we discern. And there is more within us than has yet been revealed. Let us together seek the stream of living water.

PRAYER OF CONFESSION

God of the majestic and the mundane, we are thirsty and have no cup, for we have lived without faith. Our sighs hide your still small voice, and the larger vistas of your activity are concealed from us by our obsession with proofs. Pardon our feeble trust and forgive our low expectations. We long to discern your presence in our daily encounters and to be lifted up to your Holy Way. Come, Everlasting One, to recreate us. Amen.

ASSURANCE OF FORGIVENESS

The deserts will bloom, and the eyes of the blind will be opened to see their beauty. The rains will come, and the ears of the deaf will be unstopped to hear their whispers. The earth shall bring forth its precious fruits, and we will have the strength to share in an abundant harvest. God makes all things new—even us.

COLLECT

In the midst of our hurry and impatience we seek the living water of your word, O God. Out of our blindness, weakness, and fear we bring our doubts and our faith to this moment of encounter with your truth. May your good news open our eyes, loosen our tongues, and equip our lives to share what we have seen and heard. Amen.

OFFERTORY PRAYER

Generous and Patient God, you have redeemed us and restored all our senses and abilities. Because we can see and hear your good news we would reach out to others, that you may touch them through us. We have tasted your refreshing waters and smelled the freshness of new life in your presence. So we bring our gifts and ourselves to share in your transforming work among us and in all the world. Amen.

COMMISSION AND BLESSING

Leap and sing for joy! God's promises are true.
  Our limitations are overcome in Christ.
We join the chorus of praise and thanksgiving,
  for gladness reigns in place of sorrow.
We have been saved and equipped to serve.
  God gives us strength to triumph over fear.
Jesus Christ, the One sent from God,
  has set free the possibilities within us.
Meet the coming week with fresh awareness,
  for the Sovereign One walks with you.
The way of Christ has been prepared for us.
  We will invite others to join us on God's paths.
Amen. **Amen.**

Fourth Sunday of Advent

Old Testament: Isaiah 7:10–17
Psalm 24
Epistle: Romans 1:1–7
Gospel: Matthew 1:18–25

CALL TO WORSHIP

We who seek signs and put God to the test
  are summoned once more to God's house.
We want assurances in this fragile existence,
  protection and rewards for our faithfulness.
God does not bargain with us or play favorites,
  but the gift of Emmanuel is available to all.
It is often hard to know that God is with us,

or to see how this makes any difference.
God's grace is real. We are called to be saints,
   privileged to serve as apostles among all nations.
How shall we handle God's expectations
   or respond to the Sovereign One in our midst?
Do not be afraid!   God's salvation comes to us as we are.
Come, O come, Emmanuel,
   that we may know the fulfillment you intend for us.

INVOCATION

Amazing God, we do not understand your ways, but we are drawn to
worship you. Our world crashes in on us in ways that make us feel alone
and afraid. Come to us that we may discern right from wrong and have
the strength to choose what is good and true. Equip us as we worship to
make choices and follow where you would lead us. Amen.

CALL TO CONFESSION

God must grow weary of our doubts and questions, our unconscious
reception of our Creator's good gifts, our intolerance of sisters and brothers whose experience and way of life are different from our own. Let us
open our hearts and minds to reestablish contact with the One who gives
us life.

PRAYER OF CONFESSION

O God, we have turned our backs on a simple life. Our distractions are
many and our appetites are voracious. There is no end to our desire for
things, for entertainment, for new excitement. We are self-centered and
selfish. Yet we expect you to respond to our every need and grant us
special favors. Forgive us and restore in us a love for you that helps us to
see ourselves more clearly, value the gift of life you entrust to us, and
appreciate the worth of our brothers and sisters. Amen.

ASSURANCE OF FORGIVENESS

There is good news! God's grace comes to us in Jesus Christ. We are
forgiven. We are restored to the community of faith. We are made whole
that we might do what God intends. Let us give thanks, for God's mercy
is sure, and God's purposes can be trusted.

COLLECT

God of the unexpected, meet us in these moments that new insights may
lead to faithful obedience. We would not worry you with pleas for new
signs and wonders. Only speak to us through the Word-made-flesh that
we may experience your grace and peace. Amen.

OFFERTORY PRAYER

The amazing gift of One who fully embodied your intention for humanity
prompts us to make a grateful response. In Christ we have known a love

that will not let us go. Through our offerings we would share this love in our community and to the ends of the earth. Amen.

COMMISSION AND BLESSING

Our busy world summons us back to the frantic rush;
  there are so many things to do this week!
**In the excitement of Christmas programs and activities
  we will not forget why we celebrate.**
The promise of Emmanuel is fulfilled:
  God is with us all as we go our separate ways.
**We will see God in the expectant faces of children,
  in harried parents and joyous grandparents.**
See God also in the lonely and bereaved,
  in the homeless and jobless of this and many lands.
**Emmanuel can be real to these sufferers
  if we embody the Christmas gift of love.**
Share generously as God has blessed you;
  our faithfulness is measured by our caring.
**In joyful anticipation we offer ourselves to others
  that God's salvation may find practical expression.**
Amen. **Amen.**

The Christmas Season

Christmas Eve/Day

Old Testament: Isaiah 9:2–7
  Psalm 96
Epistle: Titus 2:11–14
Gospel: Luke 2:1–20

CALL TO WORSHIP

Light dispels the shadows in which we have lived.
  A child is born; an heir is given.
We have seen the light and are afraid;
  we have seen the light and give thanks for it.
All gifts may both threaten and delight,
  for they bring change, and change upsets us.
We want to walk in the ways of peace,
  to uphold justice and righteousness.
That means giving up some advantages
  and caring enough to take risks for others.
We want to respond to those who need us,
  as the shepherds responded to the angels' song.
Let us join in worship and celebration
  that we may be equipped for every good work.
We would praise and glorify God
  and ready ourselves to share the good news.

INVOCATION

Giver of light, who breaks yokes of oppression, we rejoice at words of promise, reminding us that all oppression is a violation of your purposes. We welcome the embodiment of peace in the babe of Bethlehem. May the little child lead us and our nation to embrace those attitudes and actions that lead to true peace—peace that brings equity and opportunity for all. As we join hearts and minds in joyous worship, ready us to serve your peaceful purposes in days that follow. Amen.

COLLECT (PRAYER OF PREPARATION BEFORE THE SCRIPTURES)

We await fulfillment of your promise, O God: the child, born to be Wonderful Counselor and Prince of Peace. May the shepherds' response represent our reordered priorities. Save us from those passions that draw us away from your purposes for us, and fill us with zeal for our appointed tasks. Amen.

OFFERTORY PRAYER

We give because you have given so much to us. We give because we believe in the way of peace that Christmas proclaims. We give to build right relations among us and with you. We give to build a peaceful world. May your shalom reign here and spread through all those causes and persons whom we equip with our offerings. Amen.

COMMISSION AND BLESSING

Go forth as light-bearers and peacemakers,
heralds of God's good news to the world.
What a joy it is to be God's messengers,
to end oppression and proclaim justice.
Renounce irreligious and worldly passions,
for God sets you free from bondage to things.
How exhilarating it is to venture in new paths
without the burden of envy and greed.
Christ came as God's greatest gift,
to redeem us from all iniquity.
We venture forth, eager to do good
and live sensitive, balanced, and purpose-filled lives.
See for yourselves what God has done.
Live among others the good news of great joy.
We leave this time of worship,
glorifying and praising God
for all we have seen and heard.
Amen. **Amen.**

Christmas Day (Alternate Reading 1)

Old Testament: Isaiah 62:6–12
Psalm 97
Epistle: Titus 3:4–7
Gospel: Luke 2:8–20

CALL TO WORSHIP

Come, holy people, redeemed of God,
to follow the way prepared for you.
Glory to God in the highest,
and peace on earth among those who please God.
Once again the earth is surprised at a manger,
as the glory of God transforms the commonplace.

**Let us go to Bethlehem to see
what God has made known to us.**
Experience anew the wonder of God's ways.
Kneel in awe before life that is fresh and new.
**Let us glorify and praise God
for all that we have seen and heard!**

INVOCATION

Gracious God, whose visitation to our planet is celebrated in the birth of a child, we long to experience once again the awe and wonder of the Christmas story. We welcome our Savior, the gift of your goodness and loving-kindness. Our deeds have not warranted this outpouring of your mercy. Yet you have rescued and defended us and made us heirs in hope of eternal life. Grant us the inner conviction of your presence within and among us as we sing the carols and rejoice in our salvation. Amen.

COLLECT

Merciful God, whose salvation is for all people, lead us in these moments from hearing to responding, from immediate concerns to eternal hope, from routine pursuits to the interruption of the manger. We would join the company of the redeemed in songs of praise and the sharing of good news. Amen.

OFFERTORY PRAYER

Renewing Spirit, we have been blessed by the old, old story and a new, new outpouring of your love. We would give that love away, knowing that this is the only way we can keep it alive among us. May all that we dedicate to you now be used to express the riches of your grace to people who need good news. Amen.

COMMISSION AND BLESSING

In the quiet beauty of Christmas
the hardness of our hearts is melted.
**We have sensed truths too deep for words
and been in touch with realities beyond our reach.**
Love is especially real at Christmas,
lifting us above our indifference and hatreds.
**We want the joy and goodness to continue;
we long to be generous, caring people.**
Old selfishness and rivalries cannot survive
when people kneel together at the manger.
**We would glorify and praise God
through new attitudes and greater appreciation
of all our brothers and sisters.**

The peace of Christmas dwell with you,
  now and forever more. Amen.
Amen.

Christmas Day (Alternate Reading 2)

Old Testament: Isaiah 52:7–10
  Psalm 98
Epistle: Hebrews 1:1–12
Gospel: John 1:1–14

CALL TO WORSHIP
Break forth together into singing,
  for God has visited and comforted God's people.
**In many ways God spoke to our ancestors
  but most of all in the person of Jesus.**
How beautiful upon the mountains
  are the feet of one who brings good tidings.
**We rejoice in the One who publishes salvation
  and carries to us good news of peace.**
The Word became flesh and dwelt among us,
  full of grace and truth.
**The Word was light and life to all,
  and the darkness has not overcome it.**
Come to share the joy
  and give honor to God's name. Amen.
Amen.

INVOCATION
Reigning and Revealing One, we join your angels in worshiping the Child. This day is the work of your hands, and we rejoice. Speak to us in ways we can understand, of mysteries we cannot comprehend. We come seeking light and truth. We need your assurance and comfort. We want to be part of your salvation that reaches to the ends of the earth. May we know the Word-made-flesh so the stories of Christmas will have meaning for us. Amen.

COLLECT
Comforting and Challenging God, speak to us again through the Child who lived your Word in action beyond words. We need the good tidings of your reign among us, of light that no darkness can quench, of grace and truth that empowers us to live as your children. Amen.

OFFERTORY PRAYER

We seek to make your name known to the ends of the earth, O God of all our beginnings. We want the whole world to hear good news of peace. Bless and multiply our offerings that they may bear witness to the light. Amen.

COMMISSION AND BLESSING

Whatever burdens you carried to this worship,
   leave them behind, to face the world anew.
Timeless truth has broken into our earthly days,
   so many of our worries can be discarded.
Whatever sadness envelops you in this season
   is being transcended and turned to good ends.
We have known the comfort of God's presence
   and the healing touch of God's grace.
Whatever doubts have held you captive
   and cut off encounter with the Eternal
   surrender to the One who is ever the same,
   yet makes all things new.
All the ends of the earth shall see
   the salvation of our God.
Carry forth into the world and into coming days
   the joy and peace of Christmas.
We seek to be light-bearers
   amid all the shadows along life's pathways.
Amen. Amen.

First Sunday After Christmas

Old Testament: Isaiah 63:7–9
                Psalm 111
Epistle: Hebrews 2:10–18
Gospel: Matthew 2:13–15, 19–23

CALL TO WORSHIP

The Christmas season continues,
   and the spirit of Christmas reigns among us.
We want to prolong the friendly greetings
   and carols of good cheer.
The steadfast love of God
   abides with all who are receptive to it.

We want to stay in familiar places,
   enjoying God's mercy and redemption.
The same God who meets us here
   sends us to far places for our safety and growth.
We will not turn away from any possibilities
   God has in store for us.
The One by whom and for whom all things exist
   welcomes us as sisters and brothers of Jesus.
In the name of one who shared our humanity,
   we bring our worship and praise.

INVOCATION

We meet in the name of Jesus Christ, who welcomes us as sisters and brothers. We come in trust, knowing that you will help us to face life's temptations and overcome them, believing that you will see us through times of suffering and affliction, confident that you will never break covenant with us. Thank you for your faithfulness, kindness, and mercy to us as we seek to respond in obedience and loving service. Amen.

COLLECT

God of steadfast love and justice, we approach your word with both childlike trust and maturing eyes of faith. Set us free from all that would keep us from hearing and responding to the message you intend for us. In the name of our merciful and faithful high priest, Jesus Christ. Amen.

OFFERTORY PRAYER

What shall we give to the One who destroys the power of death and sin? How can we give thanks for the Supportive Presence who lifts us up and carries us when all else fails? We present these offerings as our response, rejoicing in your covenant with us. Thank you for accepting and affirming whatever we have to give. Amen.

COMMISSION AND BLESSING

God, who brings you to the glory of a living faith,
   empowers you now to live with integrity.
We put our trust in God,
   fearing no one and no circumstance.
Jesus Christ, who shared our human nature,
   delivers us from all bondage.
We are free to love and serve
   without deception or selfish concern.
Temptation holds no power over us
   and suffering presents no threat.
We are united in the love of Christ,
   whose brothers and sisters we are.

God's mercy and peace go with you,
    transforming every day with joy.
We have been prepared by love
    to give our best, wherever we go.
Amen. **Amen.**

January 1—New Year's Day

Old Testament: Deuteronomy 8:1–10
                  Psalm 117
Epistle: Revelation 21:1–6a
Gospel: Matthew 25:31–46

CALL TO WORSHIP
The dwelling place of God is with humanity.
    The Human One comes among us in glory.
We will be God's people,
    acknowledging God's presence with us.
God is making all things new.
    Praise God, all nations!
Great is God's steadfast love,
    and God's faithfulness endures forever.
Praise God in word and in deed.
    Praise God in your attitudes and actions.
We meet God in the hungry and thirsty,
    in the stranger and sufferer.
God is at work in you,
    and God is served through your efforts.
We rejoice in the opportunity to reach out
    to sisters and brothers in need.
Amen. **Amen.**

INVOCATION
We welcome the new beginning that a fresh year offers. All our good
intentions are caught up in the promise of starting over. Help us to leave
behind that which we cannot change and move forward boldly on the
paths in which you would lead us. We accept from your hand the water of
life. May the fountain of love never run dry, for we need to drink from it
day after day. Amen.

COLLECT
Bring us, O God, to your new heaven and new earth. In humility we
recognize that you feed us with bread and the bread of life. You clothe us,

16 The Christmas Season

discipline us, and grant us a friendly dwelling place. And we, in turn, are called to pass on your gifts. Tell us again of your intentions for us. Amen.

OFFERTORY PRAYER

May our offerings provide manna in the wilderness for those who hunger, pure water for many who must walk miles for its cool refreshment, shelter for the homeless, clothing for the naked, a welcome for the friendless, and a faith to make sense out of life. If our gifts are to accomplish all you intend, we must multiply our generosity and depend on you to accomplish far more than we have any right to expect. Bless each gift and giver, we pray in Jesus' name. Amen.

COMMISSION AND BLESSING

Ours is a good land of fountains and springs,
of good harvests and multiple resources.
Renew our appreciation of our blessings, O God,
and enhance our stewardship.
Remember the goodness of God
and the expectation in God's commandments.
Help us to hear the still small voice
that echoes through all our encounters.
God is the Alpha and Omega, beginning and end.
You cannot hide or stray from God's attention.
Hear our cries, O God, attend to our pain,
and alert us to the needs of others.
God chooses to dwell with us
and meet human need through us.
Grant us the resources and the will
to live this year as you intend.
Amen. **Amen.**

January 1—Celebration of Jesus and Mary

Old Testament: Numbers 6:22–27
Psalm 67
Epistle: Galatians 4:4–7 or Philippians 2:9–13
Gospel: Luke 2:15–21

CALL TO WORSHIP

Let all the people praise you, O God;
let all the people praise you.
Be gracious to us, O God, and bless us,
and make your face shine on us.

May God's way be known on earth,
  God's saving power among all nations.
Let the nations be glad and sing for joy,
  for God judges the people with equity.
The earth has yielded its increase;
  God, our God, has blessed us.
God has blessed us more than we know or deserve;
  let all the ends of the earth tremble
  and bow down in awe and praise.
Amen. **Amen.**

INVOCATION

We celebrate again Christ's coming into the world, born of Mary, subject to the law, to live as one of us. As we feel again the amazement of the shepherds, move us to bow our knees and sing our confession of praise. With fear and trembling, we claim the salvation that Christ brings. Engage us in the responses that will heal us and equip us to share good news. Amen.

COLLECT

As we hear the stories of old, bring us into the presence of the holy family, through whom we have recognized all humanity as our brothers and sisters. Be at work in us to accomplish that which is your will for us. Amen.

OFFERTORY PRAYER

Generous and Loving God, your gift in the manger is a mystery that time and growing understanding only deepen. You have made us heirs of your abundance, in this life and beyond. Surely, our greatest privilege is to return as much as we can of all you entrust to us. Increase our generosity and our joy in giving. Amen.

COMMISSION AND BLESSING

Hurry into the world to observe God's miracles,
  which happen in the most unexpected places.
God is at work wherever slaves are freed,
  visions are seen, and new life appears.
When we accept our adoption into God's family
  we become storytellers and miracle-workers.
We are made certain of our salvation,
  in the healing love we receive and share.
Tell the world a Savior has come!
We have good news to share!
"The Lord bless you and keep you:
  The Lord make God's face shine on you,
  and be gracious to you:

The Lord lift up God's countenance upon us,
and grant us peace."
Amen. **Amen.**

Second Sunday After Christmas

Old Testament: Jeremiah 31:7–14
Psalm 147:12–20
Epistle: Ephesians 1:3–6, 15–23
Gospel: John 1:1–18

CALL TO WORSHIP
Praise God who has blessed us in Christ
with every spiritual blessing.
We cannot keep silent,
for our lives have been warmed and affirmed.
In the depth of our spirits
we have seen new meaning and purpose for our days.
Our eyes have been enlightened,
and we have been called to a new hope.
The anguish of our times and threats of extinction
are not the prevailing word.
Christ, who is head of all things, leads the way
against all who would hurt and destroy.
Come, then, with shouts of praise and gladness,
rejoicing that God saves and gathers us together.
God keeps us as a shepherd keeps a flock
and grants us power to be God's own children.
Amen. **Amen.**

INVOCATION
Eternal God, active in human history on this chosen planet, we give thanks for your visitation in our midst. For the old, old story we have relived in this Christmas season we sing our gratitude. Continue with us, God of our salvation, that we may receive wisdom and grow in love toward all your saints. May your Word-made-flesh herald a renewal among us. To that end, bless this time of worship, in Jesus' name. Amen.

COLLECT
Persuading Spirit, whose power has gathered your people from the far corners of the earth, we long for your active presence among us and within. Lead us and enlighten us, that we may be radiant and alive in our work as the body of Christ among all people. Amen.

OFFERTORY PRAYER

As we present our offerings, O God, we pray that your investment in us will yield exciting dividends. What we return for the work of your church is only a portion of all we would contribute to the cause of righteousness and peace. We seek to devote the full riches of our inheritance from your hand to the accomplishment of your purposes among all nations. Amen.

COMMISSION AND BLESSING

Return to your places of habitation
  with strengthened limbs and opened eyes.
**God has put a new and right spirit
  within us and among us.**
Your devotion is pleasing to the Sovereign One,
  and your faithfulness is remembered.
**We seek to dwell in awareness of God's presence,
  wherever we are, in whatever we do.**
Uphold one another in prayer
  as we seek to advance God's reign among us.
**Our prayers of thanksgiving and remembrance
  bind us to all for whom we pray.**
May every blessing rest upon you,
  God's chosen ones, as you continue in faithfulness.
**We carry a vivid awareness of God's blessing
  into a new season and a new year.**
Amen. Amen.

The Epiphany Season

Epiphany

Old Testament: Isaiah 60:1–6
Psalm 72:1–14
Epistle: Ephesians 3:1–12
Gospel: Matthew 2:1–12

CALL TO WORSHIP
Arise, shine, for your light has come,
and the glory of God has risen upon you.
We, who live in a shadowed world,
have seen God's revelation in Jesus.
Lift up your eyes and see:
God's light dwells in you and others see it.
Our hearts rejoice at the opportunity
to witness to what we have heard and observed.
Gather, then, as apostles and prophets,
stewards of the mystery of Christ.
We have seen a star
and have come to worship. *All: Let us worship God!*
May your awareness, responsiveness, and reverence
be strengthened in our time together.
We will search diligently and listen carefully
for all that God would reveal to us.
Amen. **Amen.**

Omit

INVOCATION
We gather as ministers of your good news to explore the unsearchable riches of Christ. We take seriously the mandate you have given us, to be partakers of the gospel promises and members of the body of Christ. Encounter us here with a message so compelling that we will be encouraged to confront those principalities and powers that would thwart your reign among us. Grant us boldness and confidence to follow where Christ would lead us. Amen.

COLLECT (PRAYER OF PREPARATION BEFORE THE SCRIPTURES)
Out of the shadows of our lives we seek your revelation, Glorious and Gracious God. Your light shines on the people of this planet. We feel its warmth and are caught up in the wonder of your coming to us in Jesus of Nazareth and including us in your eternal purposes. May our search lead

to renewed commitment and the joy of following those directives that are your genuine intent for us. Amen.

OFFERTORY PRAYER

As the magi presented costly gifts to the Child they dared to worship as your special messenger, we would give our best through the church, which continues as Christ's body and the carrier of good news. Keep us open to the signs of your presence and responsive to your summons, no matter where it leads. Amen.

COMMISSION AND BLESSING

Go forth into the world, emboldened and equipped
to witness to all you have seen and heard.
**Our hearts and minds thrill at the challenges
of discipleship and apostleship.**
May the radiance of your faith
inspire others to seek the Christ.
**It is an awesome thing to be entrusted
with responsibility to share the good news.**
To the least of all the saints
God's grace and power is given!
**We pray for the insight and humility
to live up to that trust.**
Amen. **Amen.**

First Sunday After Epiphany
(Baptism of Our Sovereign)

Old Testament: Isaiah 42:1–9
                     Psalm 29
Epistle: Acts 10:34–43
Gospel: Matthew 3:13–17

CALL TO WORSHIP

The One who granted us the breath of life
is present here to greet us.
**Praise God for the gift of life
and the linking of our lives with one another.**
God's own Spirit rests upon us,
drawing us into the family of faith.
**We have been baptized into Christ
and share in the mission entrusted to Jesus.**

The good news of peace is for all people,
for God shows no partiality.
**All who fear God and do what is right
are acceptable to the God of the universe.**
Come together, then, to remember Jesus' baptism
and ponder its implications for us.
**Open up your heavens to us, O God,
that your reality may be inescapably apparent.**
Amen. **Amen.**

INVOCATION

Great God, above all gods, we who fail so often and are so easily discouraged return for spiritual refreshment and practical directions. Take us by the hand and renew in us once more your holy covenant. Open the eyes that have been unable to see your truth. Release those of us who live in prisons of our own making and those bound by the sins of others. Grant us the help that we need to live freely in response to your Spirit. Amen.

COLLECT

God of justice and righteousness, we who are oppressed and oppressors pause again to hear you speak through ancient texts of things that are ever new. As we join Christ in baptism, we remember that we, too, have been baptized to be healers and peacemakers. Amen.

OFFERTORY PRAYER

Your abundant outpouring to us, O God, has included many things we have come to enjoy and take for granted. Some of these things have become for us graven images that occupy our time and attention. In this offering we are recalled to matters of first importance, and we give ourselves and our substance to them. May all that we dedicate here, including life itself, accomplish much good and bring healing to our troubled world. In Jesus' name. Amen.

COMMISSION AND BLESSING

The One who granted us the breath of life
has baptized us with water and the Spirit.
**We are supported and strengthened by God's love
and by the family of faith of which we are a part.**
Carry forward the mission that Christ entrusts to us:
proclaim peace to all people everywhere.
**Our differences are transcended
in the healing streams of God's impartiality.**
In humility, and yet with confidence,
we go out to witness to our faith.
**The truth of God has been real to us here,
and we carry with us the power of this encounter.**

The God of righteousness and justice sends us forth
to win freedom for the oppressed of the earth.
As Jesus went about healing and doing good,
we go out to extend God's covenant to all.
Amen. **Amen.**

Second Sunday After Epiphany

Old Testament: Isaiah 49:1–7
                   Psalm 40:1–11
Epistle: 1 Corinthians 1:1–9
Gospel: John 1:29–34

CALL TO WORSHIP

Grace to you and peace from God our Father and Mother,
and from the Sovereign Jesus Christ.
We hear God naming our names
and calling us to join the company of the saints.
We are God's chosen ones, valued in our uniqueness
and commissioned for service to all.
How can we be saints when our labor seems fruitless
or servants when our strength is spent for nothing?
God does not measure our success
but rather our faithfulness.
We will turn to God for the strength we need,
for greater knowledge and more eloquent speech.
You are not lacking in any spiritual gift;
God is faithful, and will provide for you. Amen.
Amen.

INVOCATION

How awesome it is, O Holy One, to sense that you have chosen us for
great responsibilities. You give us as a light to the nations, so your
salvation may reach the ends of the earth. Grant that we may reflect, and
not block, the illuminating grace you intend for all whose lives we touch
and the multitudes we will never know. We need this hour of worship to
strengthen our resolve and equip us to represent you well. Amen.

COLLECT

Mother and Father of us all, you have named us and called us to be saints.
We have received your gifts and the opportunity to follow Jesus Christ in
a vital ministry to our world. Speak to us now through words that can

meet us where we are with the Word made flesh. May we dwell with Christ, in whose name we pray. Amen.

OFFERTORY PRAYER

Before your altar we offer to you, O God, what we have to give. Some of us have few financial resources, but we return a portion to accomplish your work through this church. Few among us are biblical scholars, but we come together to learn. Eloquent testimony to our faith is beyond the reach of many of us, but we recognize that often a simple honest word to others is sufficient to draw them nearer to your healing power. You have promised that we shall not be lacking in any spiritual gift. These we bring for your blessing. May our offerings equip us to serve wherever you call. Amen.

COMMISSION AND BLESSING

You have been equipped for your life of service
    far beyond your testing of that equipment.
We are amazed that God chooses us
    and assures us of the strength we need for each task.
God's promises are not empty rhetoric;
    God is a constant presence and faithful support.
When we are discouraged we will not give up
    but will return to the source of all life.
When we fail God, others, and our own best selves
    God's love continues to uphold and strengthen us.
God sustains us when times are most difficult
    and renews us through our faith community.
Reenter your everyday world with confidence.
    The heavens have opened to bless you.
Grace to us and peace from God, our Mother and Father,
    and from the Sovereign Jesus Christ.
Amen. Amen.

Third Sunday After Epiphany

Old Testament: Isaiah 9:1–4
                Psalm 27:1–6
Epistle: 1 Corinthians 1:10–17
Gospel: Matthew 4:12–23

CALL TO WORSHIP

Come together, people of God,
    out of the gloom and shadow of a troubled world.

We come with joy to the great light
  that God has given us in Jesus Christ.
Come away, people of God,
  from the jealous rivalries that mar your days.
We come in sorrowful repentance
  to confront and overcome all that divides us.
Come to worship, people of God,
  leaving behind all else that compels your attention.
We come to refocus our priorities
  and to become more alert to God's action among us.
Amen. Amen.

INVOCATION

Sovereign God, whose activity in our everyday world we have failed to
discern, confront us here with realities we have missed. May we find new
joy in all the ways you have blessed us. May we seek compelling challenge in the opportunities you set before us. Break down the barriers we
have created among ourselves, and against you, so others may be drawn
to your lifesaving love. Amen.

COLLECT

Beyond the cries of narrow self-interest and party loyalties, we come to
hear again the summons of Jesus, "Follow me!" We ask not for eloquence
or prophetic power, but only that we might be inspired to proclaim the
gospel of God's realm in our daily living. Amen.

OFFERTORY PRAYER

With the daring of the early disciples, we present our offerings in direct
response to Christ's appeal to leave all and follow. We are withholding
much of what we possess, for we do not yet know how to live without it.
But we would not withhold ourselves—our devotion, our time, our
talents, our commitment to faithful service. Use us, as you use these
material offerings, to bring the gospel of your realm to all people everywhere. Amen.

COMMISSION AND BLESSING

God has broken through the bonds
  that keep us from realizing our own best selves.
We depart with joy in our hearts
  and the intent to live by the best we know.
God breaks the rod of all oppressors
  so they and all whom they hurt may find new life.
We are set free from bondage
  to accept the challenge of responsible freedom.
God forges the differences we express
  into new and stronger unities.

26   The Epiphany Season

We put away quarreling and strife,
    determined to listen more and speak less.
God summons us to follow Christ
    and invites all men and women to discipleship.
We assign all else to second place
    to live by God's law of love for all.
Amen. Amen.

Fourth Sunday After Epiphany

Old Testament: Micah 6:1–8
                   Psalm 37:1–11
Epistle: 1 Corinthians 1:18–31
Gospel: Matthew 5:1–12

CALL TO WORSHIP

Come, all who are haughty and proud,
    who boast of your own wisdom and virtue.
**Come, all who ignore the saving acts of God
    and use religious ritual to exalt yourselves.**
Come, all who live by deceit and lies,
    whose wrongdoing has no inner corrective.
**Come, all who are weak, lowly, and despised,
    who dare not challenge the powerful.**
All of us are summoned to this hour of worship.
    Come, as you are, to meet your God.
**We come to the Source of Life to plead our case
    and to find truth by which to live.**
Amen. Amen.

INVOCATION

All-knowing God, we gather from many different places and experiences, each with individual problems and needs. Some of us doubt our own worth and shrink from any contact that might reveal our inner poverty. Others among us have been fooling ourselves with pious pretensions and false pride. Some are bewildered and afraid while others are confident of their superior achievements and value. You bring us to a common place and present us with a Savior who embodies wisdom, righteousness, and redemption. We long to be among those who are being saved, who are learning to live a truly blessed life, who are discovering the power of God in the simple and commonplace. May this service be a time of transformation for each of us, and all of us together. Amen.

COLLECT

Melt away our false pride, O God of the weak and despised, that we may listen and hear your way of righteousness and peace. Bless us with the capacity to understand and act according to your purposes. We would walk humbly with you and the meek and lowly of the earth. Amen.

OFFERTORY PRAYER

We offer these gifts, O God, not because you require them, but because we want to express our gratitude. They are not meant to impress, but to accomplish some good in the world. With them we commit ourselves to justice, kindness, and a humble walk with our Creator. Teach us to give without counting the cost, in Jesus' name. Amen.

COMMISSION AND BLESSING

Carry with you today the wisdom and strength
   that the world calls foolish and weak.
We look from the manger to the cross
   to find redemption and sense life's meaning.
Blessed are the meek and the humble-minded.
   Blessed are the merciful and the peacemakers.
Mourners shall find comfort
   and the pure in heart shall see God.
Those who hunger and thirst for righteousness
   shall be satisfied.
Those who are persecuted and reviled
   shall dwell in the realm of heaven.
Rejoice and be glad, for God is with us
   in all the difficult places of life.
Jesus Christ, the power and wisdom of God,
   is our refuge and our strength.
Amen. Amen.

Fifth Sunday After Epiphany

Old Testament: Isaiah 58:3–9a
                   Psalm 112:4–9
Epistle: 1 Corinthians 2:1–11
Gospel: Matthew 5:13–16

CALL TO WORSHIP

No eye has seen nor ear heard nor heart conceived
   what God has prepared for those who love God.

We are drawn to worship by love beyond our knowing,
   by the secret and hidden wisdom of God.
God comes among us and within each one,
   inviting us to be salty Christians.
We are each important to the good work
   God seeks to accomplish with and through us.
We are called to be lights in the world
   and to let our lights shine brightly.
God expects us to reflect eternal truth
   and lead others to Christ's way.
With the humility of the apostle Paul,
   we offer our weakness and limited insight.
In our worship and in our service
   we seek to demonstrate the Spirit of Christ.

INVOCATION

Sovereign God, when we seek in you an Indulgent Parent, we come face to face with your high expectations for us. You meet us, not in flights of speculation, but in the everyday circumstances of our lives, inviting us to act on your behalf, to feed the hungry, house the homeless, and cover the naked. You call us to use worship, not as a period of escape, but as a time of preparation to go out and light up the world. May we find our own healing as we devote ourselves to your service. In Jesus' name, Amen.

COLLECT

Powerful and Just God, take away our weakness and fear, our reliance on human wisdom, and our temptation to substitute religion for faithfulness. As we hear your word, equip us with a righteousness that reaches out to care and share and pour ourselves out for others. Amen.

OFFERTORY PRAYER

Our offerings are not meant to maintain an institution, but to enhance a ministry. The focus of our church programs and activities goes beyond our being comforted and informed. May the well-being of our sisters and brothers around the world be at the forefront of our generous and sacrificial giving. Amen.

COMMISSION AND BLESSING

Go forth into the world
   to be salt and light wherever you go.
We are the salt of the earth;
   we are the light of the world.
Live with integrity and caring,
   according to God's law of love.
We are the only Bible some will read
   and their introduction to Christ's way.

In humility, acknowledging your own weakness,
   reach out to share what you have received.
We would loose the bonds of wickedness
   and break the yoke of oppressors.
As you give to the poor and hungry,
   you will know healing for your own need.
We trust God to provide for us
   and to empower our serving.
Amen. **Amen.**

Sixth Sunday After Epiphany

Old Testament: Deuteronomy 30:15–20
                  Psalm 119:1–8
Epistle: 1 Corinthians 3:1–9
Gospel: Matthew 5:17–26

CALL TO WORSHIP

Blessed are those who seek God,
   whose hearts are set on God's commandments.
We are inheritors of God's law
   and heirs of the prophet's mission.
God's Spirit permeates our human scene,
   lifting us above our jealousies and quarreling.
We reach for the highest and best,
   for upright hearts and righteous deeds.
In all we do, God offers us choices,
   Between good and evil, between life and death.
How shall we know the ways of God
   or understand fully the choices that are ours?
In worship we encounter God's commandments
   and explore together what it means to love God.
We have turned away from life's many distractions
   to give this time to hearing and obeying our Creator.
Amen. **Amen.**

INVOCATION

Reveal yourself to us, Holy God, for we have found that human wisdom is often insufficient and sometimes gravely mistaken. Set before us your more excellent way that sees the hurt in anger as well as murder, in partisan religious loyalties as well as worldly indifference. So envelop us

here with eternal truth that we cannot easily escape or ignore your
intentions for us during the coming week. Amen.

COLLECT

Sovereign God, in whom is all wisdom and truth, we would be obedient
to the spirit, not just the letter, of your law. We wish to turn away from the
lesser gods we have allowed into our lives, that we may walk in your ways
of reconciliation, selflessness, and compassion. Amen.

OFFERTORY PRAYER

Sometimes when we bring gifts to your altar, O God, there is no joy in
our giving. We do not experience the satisfaction that usually accom-
panies involvement in your work. Help us to remember the words and
deeds that may be cutting us off from our neighbors and blocking our full
participation in this divine and human drama of sharing. Give us the
insight and courage to seek forgiveness and accomplish reconciliation.
Then giving can once again be an exhilarating adventure. Amen.

COMMISSION AND BLESSING

God's spirit has been active in our midst,
   so we can advance from milk to solid food.
We seek now, in all times and places, to serve the One
   whom we have worshiped in these moments together.
Choose life and good, not death and evil,
   for your own sake and for all who come after you.
We would love God with our whole being,
   obey God's voice and cleave to God in all circumstances.
The gifts we have received from God's hands
   are to be shared with others.
God's truth is becoming so much a part of us
   that our lives reflect what we have seen and heard.
Be reconciled with those who have wronged you,
   and live up to the trust God invests in you.
God has blessed us.
   We will not betray God's trust.
Amen. Amen.

Seventh Sunday After Epiphany

Old Testament: Isaiah 49:8–13
                Psalm 62:5–12
Epistle: 1 Corinthians 3:10–11, 16–23
Gospel: Matthew 5:27–37

2/18/90

CALL TO WORSHIP

Sing for joy, O heavens, and exult, O earth;
  break forth, O mountains, into singing!
God has comforted God's people
  and will have compassion on the afflicted.
The Sovereign One has given us a covenant
  and summons us to this time together.
Each of us is a temple of God,
  a holy dwelling place for God's Spirit.
✗ In Christ we have been fed in green pastures
  and watered by living springs.
✗ **There is a place and a relationship**
  wherein our hunger and thirst are satisfied.
This is the time and place for encounter with God.
  Come in silence and in hope.
We trust in God who is our Refuge
  and pour out our hearts before our Rock and our Salvation.
all: Amen. Amen.

INVOCATION

Gracious God, you have richly provided for all our needs. Even when
times are hard and we feel forsaken, you do not desert us. You have led us
by springs of living water and forged paths for us through mountains of
difficulty. Because our needs recur, we long for this period of worship as a
time of renewal, visioning, and empowerment. We seek to be worthy of
the trust placed in us. Amen.

COLLECT

We seek wisdom beyond human folly, right relationships triumphing over
human sin, and your empowerment, O God, to build within us a temple
fit for your Spirit. We risk everything we have and are to hear what you
would say to us now. Amen.

OFFERTORY PRAYER

All we give we have first received from your hand, O God. It is our
privilege to be generous because we have been richly blessed. May the
opportunity to give turn us away from our preoccupation with getting. As
we seek to put first things first, we aspire to participation in God's realm
above all else. Amen.

COMMISSION AND BLESSING

As we have gathered to worship and learn,
  we now scatter for work and leisure.
What we have seen we want to share,
  and all we have heard we would heed.

32   The Epiphany Season

May our time together cause us to sing
and meet others with openness and charity.
**When we have been fully engaged in prayer,
others see a difference in us.**
We reenter our everyday world as a covenant people,
whose purpose is to reveal God's compassion.
**We go out to face our accommodation to the world,
seeking to simplify our responses as fools for Christ.**
Let us use our weakness to reveal God's strength,
our every deed to proclaim God's love.
**Our folly will be turned into productive service
and our trouble, to a wider caring for others.**
Amen. Amen.

Eighth Sunday After Epiphany

Old Testament: Leviticus 19:1–2, 9–18
Psalm 119:33–40
Epistle: 1 Corinthians 4:1–5
Gospel: Matthew 5:38–48

CALL TO WORSHIP

Gather for worship, you servants of Christ,
stewards of the mysteries of God.
**It is required of stewards
that they be found trustworthy.**
God brings to light that which is hidden
and discloses the purposes of our hearts.
**Our harvest of faithfulness is God's to judge
whether the needy and oppressed have been helped.**
Can a woman forget her sucking child
and have no concern for the fruit of her womb?
**Neither will God turn away from us,
God's own children by water and the Spirit.**
God's new order calls for special consideration
for the poor and those with disabling conditions.
**We are to make sure the poor have food to eat
and the blind and deaf are not oppressed.**
The love we extend to friends
is also meant for those who seem to be enemies.
Our prayers are not only for those we like,

but also for those who have wronged us.
Amen. **Amen.**

INVOCATION

In response to your love for us, Gracious God, we are learning to love our neighbors. It is hard to turn the other cheek when we are attacked or to go the second mile when others place unjust demands on us. You tell us to make friends of our enemies and pray for those who seek to do us harm. We will listen to your Word, but not without protest. Engage us here in searching ourselves and wrestling with your instructions. In Jesus' name. Amen.

COLLECT

Dwell in us, Holy God, that we may experience the joy of honest, fair, and considerate relationships. Expand our circle of love to include all who seem to be against us, that together we may build on the foundation Christ offers us for abundant living. Amen.

OFFERTORY PRAYER

We do not claim as our own the resources you ask us to set aside for the poor, Dear God. We bring a portion of your bounty as a solemn trust and awesome privilege. While we invest only part of our resources in the outreach of this church, we also bring for your examination all our dealings with neighbors around the world who help to put food on our tables and make our lives comfortable. Help us to right any injustice from which we may be benefiting. Amen.

COMMISSION AND BLESSING

We are sent into the world
  to extend God's love in word and deed.
Because we love, the hungry have hope
  and the oppressed are set free.
The great and the lowly sit down together
  and find common enterprises to undertake.
Hatred is put down, sins are forgiven,
  and we refuse to bear grudges.
Prayers for our enemies begin the healing within us
  and extend it to those we have hated.
How good it is to go beyond the law's requirements,
  to overcome evil with good.
Amen. **Amen.**

Last Sunday After Epiphany
(Transfiguration)

Old Testament: Exodus 24:12–18
Psalm 2:6–11
Epistle: 2 Peter 1:16–21
Gospel: Matthew 17:1–9

CALL TO WORSHIP

Come to the mountaintop, all God's people;
leave all else behind to reach out to the Eternal.
How shall we climb the mountain when we cannot walk
or reach spiritual heights while weighed down with cares?
In Christ, God brings the mountaintop to us
and meets us, even in the depths of despair.
· **We see a lamp shining in a dark place,**
and the morning star rises in our hearts.
Pay attention to the signs through which God speaks;
for those with discernment, they are everywhere.
The dazzling splendor of God's glory is real,
even to those who have no eyes.
Like a devouring fire, the Spirit sweeps through our midst,
and we are transformed in its glow.
Let us come without fear or thoughts of favor,
opening ourselves to all God has in store for us.

INVOCATION

We bring our deepest longings, our bewilderment, and our complaints
into your Majestic Presence. As you encompass us in the brilliant light of
your limitless power and boundless love, our self-centered concerns are
put in perspective. We recognize Christ in our midst, the Word made
flesh. In that recognition your intentions for our lives become clearer. But
what is clear on the mountaintop becomes distorted and indistinct in the
valleys of our everyday problems. Stay with us, Sovereign One, to save us
from ourselves. Amen.

COLLECT

God of the mountains and the valleys of our lives, we wait here, in this
place apart, to hear and see your glory. Whether you come in dazzling
light or quiet word, help us to interpret aright your message for us and
our world. Amen.

OFFERTORY PRAYER

When your glory expands our horizons and we learn to identify with all whom you love, this time of sharing becomes the most important occasion in our lives. Move us beyond our own limited interpretation of your action in our midst, O God. In awe and anticipation we offer ourselves and our substance toward the fulfillment of your divine law among humankind. Amen.

COMMISSION AND BLESSING

The vision of the mountaintop is ours to tell,
  and in the valleys of everyday, people need it.
How shall we tell others of our experience
  without seeming arrogant or unbalanced?
Christ, whom we meet on life's mountaintops,
  was never pretentious amid the lowly.
In genuine caring and humble service
  we give and receive God's love in Christ.
Listen to God's beloved Child:
  "Rise and have no fear."
We depart with renewed energy and purpose
  to live God's truth among all we meet.
Amen. **Amen.**

The Season of Lent

Ash Wednesday

Old Testament: Joel 2:1–2, 12–17a
 Psalm 51:1–12
Epistle: 2 Corinthians 5:20b—6:10
Gospel: Matthew 6:1–6, 16–21

CALL TO WORSHIP
Come, people of God, to know again who you are.
 Return to the One who gives you life.
We come as children of God,
 longing for a closer walk with our Creator.
Today, salvation is offered to all who will receive it,
 gifts of healing and new life to all who accept them.
To dare to open our lives to God,
 to claim the wholeness Christ intends for us.
Those called by Christ are commissioned to serve;
 all who receive forgiveness are to live God's love.
We receive God's gifts to strengthen us
 and to equip us to reach out in love to others.
Let this be the theme of all our worship,
 the love of God, our motivation to serve.
We come with joy, expecting to be renewed:
 eager to be a channel of God's blessing.

CALL TO CONFESSION
Paul wrote to the Corinthians, "Behold, now is the acceptable time. Behold, now is the day of salvation." These words remind us of our tendency to procrastinate. Tomorrow is always soon enough to think seriously about life and its meaning. Not so. This present moment comes to us as a gift. It is the only time we know will be ours for serious reflection and genuine commitment. Let us come to God as we are, recognizing how unworthy we are to approach the One who embraces the universe, yet believing we are known and welcomed in this Awesome Presence. Let us confess our sin.

PRAYER OF CONFESSION
O Sovereign One, we have relied on the treasures of earth for our meaning. When they do not satisfy we try to fill the void with more things. We cling to our possessions as if they could save us and embrace our own customs and habits as if there were no other way. Our faith is

37

secondhand and our prayer life is narrow and unfocused. We settle for appearances rather than for substance, for looking good rather than for doing good. Someday we want to change, to embrace a better way. But it is hard to adopt new patterns, risk renewal, and commit ourselves to the one whose devotion led to a cross. We reach for the forgiveness and courage you alone can give. Save us from ourselves and our poor choices. Let today be different, a time when your love reaches us as never before and unites us with your purposes for us. In Jesus' name. Amen.

ASSURANCE OF FORGIVENESS

Salvation has come to you this day. God's reconciling love meets you where you are and welcomes you into the family. The Creator has heard the quiet longing in your hearts that no words can describe and offers healing. You are valued, each and every one, as the person you are and as the fulfilled human being you are becoming. The treasures of God's grace are yours; receive them and rejoice. Amen.

COLLECT (PRAYER OF PREPARATION BEFORE THE SCRIPTURES)

O God, you have called your people to a time of fasting and repentance. At the beginning of the lenten season we seek for ourselves those disciplines of body, mind, and spirit that will help us embrace the reconciling ministry of Christ as our own. Grant that in quietness and confidence, not in outward show, we may use this season to lay up treasures in heaven. Move us beyond self-concern to genuine regard and eager partnership with all your children everywhere. Amen.

OFFERTORY PRAYER OF DEDICATION

We bring these gifts, O God, not to win your favor, but to participate in your work of salvation in our midst. We are grateful for the opportunity to bear witness to the love we have received from your hand. In joy we dedicate ourselves anew as your servants. May these offerings and our lives spread good news, in Christ's name. Amen.

COMMISSION AND BLESSING

Go forth, people of God, to be a blessing
    to the world, in Christ's service.
We will put no obstacle in anyone's way,
    so no fault may be found with our ministry.
Let your love be genuine, your speech truthful,
    your relationship with others patient and kind.
We seek to be authentic witnesses
    to God's love in Christ Jesus.
You may face hardships, humiliation, and sorrow;
    others may not understand your commitment.

We will rejoice, even in times of difficulty:
God, in Christ, gives us all we need.
God empowers you to walk in faith and humility,
to give generously and unselfishly.
We go out to invest the gifts of God
for the sake of all whom we meet.
Amen. Amen.

First Sunday of Lent

Old Testament: Genesis 2:4b–9, 15–17, 25—3:7
Psalm 130
Epistle: Romans 5:12–19
Gospel: Matthew 4:1–11

CALL TO WORSHIP

Come, people of God, to know again who you are,
return to the One who gives you life.
We come as children of God,
longing for a closer walk with our Creator.
The abundant grace of God
is offered to all of us in Christ Jesus.
We gather to receive that gift,
to learn and remember how best to use it.
We cannot live by bread alone;
life is intended to be more than food.
Our worship is the opening of ourselves
to receive the gifts of the Spirit.
Let nothing distract you from that intent;
we have assembled that God may speak to us.
We wait upon God, the Sovereign One,
who knows us as we are and loves us.

CALL TO CONFESSION

The apostle Paul reminded members of the church at Rome that all human beings are sinners. We all give our loyalty to goals and purposes that fall far short of the will of God. We are all tempted, as was Jesus, to live by society's standards, to substitute material gain for spiritual integrity, to call attention to ourselves rather than take our place within the body of Christ, to align ourselves with the power brokers of our day rather than recognize a Higher Power over all things. Let us come to

God, recognizing how unworthy we are to approach the One who embraces the universe, yet believing we are known and welcomed in this Awesome Presence. Let us confess our sin.

PRAYER OF CONFESSION

God of all time and space, we have joined our ancestors in seeking to live our own way. We have been tempted to play God with our own lives and those of others. We have confused freedom with self-indulgence. We have sought to make decisions that are not ours to make. We have put down others to gain status for ourselves or have accepted the hierarchies of this world as God-given when they are not. Forgive us, O God, and equip us for clear thinking, honest response, and loving service. In Jesus' name. Amen.

ASSURANCE OF FORGIVENESS

The abundance of God's grace is freely given to you this day. In Christ, we have known the reign of God's righteousness. God also lives in us. Receive this gift, with joy and thanksgiving, praising God for the new life that is yours.

COLLECT

O God, we are filled with wonder as we ask about our beginnings, as we question the evil in our world, as we ponder the mystery of who you are and how we can fulfill your intent for us. Let your Word flow through these words of scripture, that we may hear what you want us to hear. As Jesus overcame the temptation to hear less than your will in verses quoted to him, may we also be empowered to reject false messages and embrace your truth. Amen.

OFFERTORY PRAYER OF DEDICATION

Through our offerings, O God, we would supply bread to those who hunger and the bread of life to feed all who need spiritual nourishment. We who have received good news seek to live by it and to share the gospel with others. May our gifts and our lives proclaim your rule among all people, beginning in our midst and extending through all your world. Amen.

COMMISSION AND BLESSING

Go forth, people of God, assured of God's grace,
   living in obedience to God's will and way.
We will not live by bread alone,
   but by the word of God, as Christ lived it.
The Christian way is not one of pride and superiority
   but of loving service and sacrifice.
We will not tempt the Sovereign One
   by seeking danger to prove God's care for us.

God does not call us to a position of power
   or provide an easy way for those who are faithful.
We will worship the One and Only God,
   revealed to us in Jesus Christ.
We have met God in this service of worship.
   Let us walk with God in service to the world.
We have received the blessing of God,
   to enrich and empower our loving and serving.
Amen. **Amen.**

Second Sunday of Lent

Old Testament: Genesis 12:1–8
                       Psalm 33:18–22
Epistle: Romans 4:1–5, 13–17
Gospel: John 3:1–17

CALL TO WORSHIP
Come, people of God, to know again who you are,
   return to the One who gives you life.
We come as children of God,
   longing for a closer walk with our Creator.
We are called to lay aside previous assumptions,
   to give up our advantages and security.
It is frightening to venture into the unknown,
   to live by faith rather than by sight.
The God who has given us life
   offers us a new birth—a new way.
We are both attracted and repelled by newness,
   by the promises and challenges of a life of faith.
Let us venture together,
   daring to feel the winds of God's Spirit.
We will join in exploring God's purposes
   and open ourselves to God's leading.

CALL TO CONFESSION
Some of us break the rules for right living and know we are sinners.
Others keep all the rules but realize that our relationships with God and
others are not really as they should be. Some of us think of ourselves
more highly than we ought to think. Others do not appreciate our own
worth as God's children, nor live in the confidence of God's love. Most of
us, when faced with a choice between security and venturing in dan-

gerous, unknown paths where God may be calling us, are reluctant to take the risks of faith. All of us are invited to name our sins and seek God's forgiveness. Let us come to God as we are, recognizing how unworthy we are to approach the One who embraces the universe, yet believing that we are known and welcomed in this Awesome Presence. Let us confess our sin.

CONFESSION OF SIN

Gracious and Loving God, you have blessed us abundantly with material and spiritual resources, but we have wasted them, complained of our lot, and asked for more benefits and protection. We have considered the things we have as our due; they are ours, to be used for our own benefit. It is hard to hear the message that all we have, even life itself, belongs to you and is to be invested in your service. When you call us to depart from our safe places to serve you or to give up our wealth for the sake of others, we are frightened. We turn away from the cost of discipleship, seeking to enjoy the benefits of faith without opening ourselves to its risks and challenges. Forgive us, O God, and give us the courage of our convictions. We pray in Jesus' name. Amen.

ASSURANCE OF FORGIVENESS

Hear the promises that come to us from God through ancient words of faith:
"Blessed are those whose iniquities are forgiven,
    and whose sins are covered;
blessed are those against whom the Sovereign One
    will not reckon their sin."
Again, it is written,
"God so loved the world that God gave God's only Child, that whoever believes in that Child should not perish but have eternal life. For God sent that Child into the world, not to condemn the world, but that through that Child the world might be saved."
We can step into the unknown in the faith that God goes with us and provides for us. Praise be to God!

COLLECT

O Sovereign One, we would enter the adventure of faithful living with pioneers of the faith. With Abraham and Sarah, we open ourselves to your call into unknown places and among unfamiliar persons. Help us to trust you enough that we will not shrink from the challenges presented to the rich young ruler. We await your word with eager attention. Amen.

OFFERTORY PRAYER

God of all humankind, send our generous gifts where we are unable to go. Send us to places where we would not venture to witness to your love,

except by the assurance of your presence with us. We rededicate all we
have and all we are to your service. Amen.

COMMISSION AND BLESSING

Truly, truly, I say to you:
"Unless you are born anew,
you cannot see the realm of God."
**We have received new life this day
and want to embrace all it may hold for us.**
The winds of God have swept through our midst
and we are caught up in the movement.
**We want to follow where Jesus would lead us,
to minister in Christ's name in our world.**
Begin where you are, remembering and applying
all you have seen and heard.
**We will relate to family, friends, and co-workers
as persons valued and loved by God.**
Dare to change your living and giving habits,
to decide and act today in newness of life.
**We have received power to grow and change:
we accept this new venture of faith
as God's gift to us. Thanks be to God!**
Amen. Amen.

Third Sunday of Lent

Old Testament: Exodus 17:3–7
                   Psalm 95
Epistle: Romans 5:1–11
Gospel: John 4:5–42

CALL TO WORSHIP

Come, people of God, to know again who you are,
return to the One who gives you life.
**We come as children of God,
longing for a closer walk with our Creator.**
Come, all who are thirsty for living water.
Open yourselves to the One who supplies it.
**We would drink this day from the spiritual depths,
seeking to know and experience life's meaning.**
Gather as people of faith, embracing renewal,
eager for reconciliation with God and humankind.

We have assembled to hear for ourselves
   the good news Christ brings to all people.
God meets and accepts us where we are,
   helping us to know ourselves as we are known.
We will worship with enthusiastic expectation,
   anticipating salvation in our lives and relationships.

CALL TO CONFESSION

In the Bible we encounter persons whose memories were short when it came to remembering all God's blessings or recalling their own unfaithfulness. These same people could recount every moment of suffering, every time when God seemed to fail them, all those situations in which life seemed unfair. We are a lot like our biblical ancestors. Like them, we need a broader view of divine majesty and our own place in creation. Let us come to God, recognizing how unworthy we are to approach the One who embraces the universe, yet believing we are known and welcomed in this Awesome Presence. Let us confess our sin.

PRAYER OF CONFESSION

God of all majesty and power, we bring to you all our complaints and our hopes, our sadness and our joys, our fears and our faith. We have deplored your absence when we have needed help, your unresponsiveness when our hearts cried out for assurance, your unfairness when we have suffered losses and disappointments. How can we believe in you, O God? And how can you love us? We have been quick to excuse our own faithlessness and slow to acknowledge your continuing patience and generosity. We have used religion to divert attention from our waywardness, and pretensions of righteousness as a substitute for genuine commitment. Have mercy on us, O God, as we bare our souls before your throne of grace. Grant us the capacity to change for the better and the will to do our part to accomplish that change, in Jesus' name. Amen.

ASSURANCE OF FORGIVENESS

Hear God's word of forgiveness as it comes to us through the experience of our religious forebears:
"While we were still weak, at the right time,
   Christ died for the ungodly . . .
while we were enemies we were reconciled to God
   by the death of God's Own Child . . .
through Jesus Christ, we have now received
   reconciliation with God."
Believe these words! Live by them! God, in Christ, is empowering you for a new life of faithfulness and service. Amen.

COLLECT

Open the scriptures to us, O God, that we may see ourselves in the stories and hear both a word of encouragement and a word of challenge.

Strengthen our faith by opening all our senses to an awareness of your action on our behalf. Come to us in our weakness, our self-justification, our arrogance, or our self-deprecation. Meet us at the point of our own special needs and speak your word to us. Amen.

OFFERTORY PRAYER

These gifts express our gratitude for your lavish outpouring of love in Jesus Christ and your generous provision for all our needs. We dedicate our tithes and offerings for use in the fields that are ripe for harvest. May this money, along with our words and deeds, make an effective witness to Jesus Christ as the Savior of the World. Amen.

COMMISSION AND BLESSING

We have been together to worship God, in spirit and truth,
    to find refreshing water and nourishing food.
We have received "springs of living water,"
and "our food is to do the will of God."
In our separate places at home and at work,
    God continues to supply our every need.
We will take time to be nourished by God
and will seek to share God's gifts with others.
"Rejoice in your suffering,
    knowing that suffering produces endurance.
Endurance produces character, character produces hope,
and hope does not disappoint us.
God's love has been poured into our hearts
    through the Holy Spirit which has been given to us."
We receive God's Spirit to empower our living,
one day at a time, through the coming week.
Amen. Amen.

Fourth Sunday of Lent

Old Testament: 1 Samuel 16:1–13
                  Psalm 23
Epistle: Ephesians 5:8–14
Gospel: John 9:1–41

CALL TO WORSHIP

Come, people of God, to know again who you are;
    return to the One who gives you life.
We come as children of God,
    longing for a closer walk with our Creator.

Come, all who see your own weakness and imperfections,
for God is not impressed by outward appearances.
We respond to God's welcoming love
and rejoice that there is a place for us here.
Come, all who are blind but long to see,
all who stumble in the dark but yearn for light.
We are glad for this time of healing and refreshment,
this hour of celebration and enlightenment.
"Awake, O sleeper, and arise from the dead,
and Christ shall give you light."
We are alert to the surprises God has in store for us,
eager to see the new possibilities Christ offers.

all: Let us worship God!

CALL TO CONFESSION

Once again we have gathered to support one another in our common approach to the Sovereign Ruler of the universe. We who have succumbed to the subtle temptations to "play God" during another week are confronted today by the One True God, who sees through our pretenses. We who are impressed by appearances and regulated by the predictable are challenged during this lenten season to be alert to God's action in our midst. God's activity breaks through our stereotypes, our interpretations and our preferences to create new situations. The ways of God are not limited to our narrow understandings. How have we violated God's intention for us during the past week? . . .

Let us come to God as we are, recognizing how unworthy we are to approach the One who embraces the universe yet believing that we are known and welcomed in this Awesome Presence. Let us confess our sin.

PRAYER OF CONFESSION

Great God, above all gods, we confess that we have made idols of our rules and ways, our possessions and activities, our nation and loved ones. We have tried to capture you in a tame and predictable religious system, in which we come out on top and others are put down. We resist your Saving Presence as you break into our usual patterns to heal our brokenness and set us on new paths. We turn our backs on your love and refuse to take the risks of caring and trusting—the way Christ taught us to relate to others. Help us, O God, to recognize our sin and want to turn away from it. Give us the courage to change. We pray in Jesus' name. Amen.

ASSURANCE OF FORGIVENESS

Christ has come among us, opening the eyes of the blind, bringing light to those who have walked in darkness. The miracle of Christ's transforming presence is offered to you this day. Receive the gift. Walk in the light. Let the brightness of God's love shine through you. Amen.

46 The Season of Lent

COLLECT

Prepare us, O Sovereign One, to hear your word through stories told long ago. In the Bible we encounter religious leaders who made political decisions, violated the accepted order, and incurred the wrath of those in power. We ask for inspiration, motivation, and boldness to witness as effectively in our own day as they did in theirs. Speak to us now, that your Word may bear fruit in our lives. Amen.

OFFERTORY PRAYER

O God, we do not pretend that these gifts are more than small tokens of what a real offering would be. You ask for the commitment of our lives; we bring a few leftovers from the abundance of your generosity to us. Yet, for some, there is sacrifice here, for some a deep sense of appreciation and thanksgiving, for some a conviction that all we claim as our own, even life itself, belongs to you and is only loaned to us to manage for a while. Take these beginning understandings and help us to grow toward faithful stewardship of all you entrust to us. Amen.

COMMISSION AND BLESSING

God has acted to open our eyes and ears,
   to release us from the prisons of our limited perceptions.
Christ shines as a light amid our darkness,
   opening our lives to new possibilities.
The One who lived fully God's intentions for humanity
   summons us to live as authentic human beings.
We have been chosen as servants of the most high God,
   as bearers of the Spirit and mission of Christ.
Let us go forth from this place
   to do the work of Christ among all we meet.
We will serve as witnesses to the Light,
   as human beacons through whom Christ is revealed.
God's saving love goes with us to bless and empower;
   Christ sends us out as friends and representatives.
We accept Christ's commission and blessing:
   we will think and act according to God's will for us.
Amen. **Amen.**

Fifth Sunday of Lent

Old Testament: Ezekiel 37:1–14
                    Psalm 116:1–9
Epistle: Romans 8:6–19
Gospel: John 11:1–53

CALL TO WORSHIP

Come, people of God, to know again who you are.
  Return to the One who gives you life.
We come as children of God,
  longing for a closer walk with our Creator.
Gather together, all who feel spent and discouraged,
  all who are weighed down, in bondage, and disheartened.
"Our bones are dried up, and our hope is lost."
  We feel death and decay in the midst of our days.
God's Spirit enters our "valley of dry bones"
  to call us to a time of revitalizing worship.
How can we sing songs of joy and praise
  when there is no life in us?
The breath of God cleanses, and hope is renewed:
  life is restored to God's children.
We welcome the winds of God among us,
  the Spirit who offers life in all its fullness.

CALL TO CONFESSION

The apostle Paul wrote to the church at Rome: "The mind that is set on the flesh is hostile to God; it does not submit to God's law, indeed it cannot . . . [but if] the Spirit of God dwells in you . . . your spirits are alive . . . [and] you are children of God." As Paul observed, we spend a lot of time as one-dimensional people. We focus on our own interests as if there were no God, and other people become no more than props in our life stories. Suddenly we are faced with meaninglessness, and we begin to feel like "dry bones." Let us come to God, recognizing how unworthy we are to approach the One who embraces the universe yet believing we are known and welcomed in this Awesome Presence. Let us confess our sin.

PRAYER OF CONFESSION

God of the living and the dead, we confess that sometimes we are more dead than alive to the possibilities you place before us. In the midst of pain, unfairness, and destructive forces on all sides, we see little hope. We find it hard to discern a role for ourselves in working for a better world; we seem powerless to change even that little part of the planet where we live. How can we find a spiritual dimension in life that would change the way we view conditions? Where do we go for the power to face and overcome a world that denies the resurrection? O God, we want to find that new life which triumphs over death and the grave. Forgive our dullness and grant us new vision and vitality. In Jesus' name. Amen.

ASSURANCE OF FORGIVENESS

"Thus says the Sovereign God, 'I will raise you from your graves, O my people; and I will bring you home. . . . I will put my Spirit within you, and you shall live. . . . I, the Sovereign One, have spoken, and I have done it,' says God." We are assured that God is already at work in our lives, accepting us where we are and granting us new life. Know that you are being unbound; you are free to live, able to share in God's saving action in our midst. Accept the gift of God's forgiveness and empowerment. Take your place among Christ's disciples. Amen.

COLLECT

In the vivid pictures of life painted by prophet, missionary, and evangelist, may we sense the movement of your Spirit, which is beyond the capacity of words to report. O God, help us to experience your transcendent power in the midst of our own lives, bringing life out of death, hope out of despair, joy out of sorrow. Help us to find life and peace, even as this season moves us toward Calvary. Amen.

OFFERTORY PRAYER

Bring life, O God, to the program and mission of this church, which we support through our tithes and offerings. May our giving bring life and hope in many "valleys of dry bones." As Christ sacrificed life for us, so may each of us commit ourselves to carrying forward the work to which we are called in our own day. Bless us and all the gifts we bring, in Jesus' name, Amen.

COMMISSION AND BLESSING

Go forth into the world, forever changed,
    freed from your narrow vision and limited faithfulness.
We have received new life:
    these dead bones live again.
Know that the God who raised Christ from the dead
    is also at work in you to bring life to others.
We have been claimed by God,
    adopted as God's own children, heirs of grace.
Share God's gift with all who are in bondage,
    longing to be unbound and set free.
We will respond in faith and action
    to God's call and our neighbor's need.
The Spirit of God dwells in you,
    empowering you for faithful service.
We welcome the winds of God to empower us,
    the love of God to inform and shape our service.
Amen. **Amen.**

Sixth Sunday of Lent
(Palm Sunday)

Old Testament: Isaiah 50:4–9a
Psalm 118:19–29
Epistle: Philippians 2:5–11
Gospel: Matthew 21:1–11

CALL TO WORSHIP

Hosanna, Child of David!
Blessed is the One who comes in the Sovereign's name!
What is this strange procession?
Why are people so excited?
The prophet has come!
The One who talks sense and listens.
But good clothes are being trampled,
and they're getting dirty underfoot.
Jesus has no concern about possessions;
but people have been healed by a touch.
Why would a prophet come here?
We like things quiet and predictable.
This is the One who saves us,
who teaches us how to live.
Will salvation bring changes I'll regret?
What will it cost to take this One seriously?

INVOCATION

We come together, as believers and skeptics, to remember the drama of
Jesus' entry into Jerusalem. We can get caught up in the excitement of a
parade, especially in an important place or honoring someone we know.
We like celebrations. But part of us holds back. We know the rest of the
story. It involves denial and betrayal, spitting and shame, a crown of
thorns, and a cruel cross. O God, it's hard to make sense out of life when
goodness is crucified and evil seems to triumph. Free us from our fear of
consequences so we, too, can wave branches and sing praises. Amen.

COLLECT

Awaken us to full attention, God, so we can hear as those who are taught.
When adversaries challenge our faith, stand by to vindicate us. Grant us
the perspective to bear cruel attacks or take enthusiastic acclaim in
stride. Keep us humble, that we may be effective witnesses to your love.
Amen.

OFFERTORY PRAYER

When you ask for what we have to give or lend, we want to offer it gladly. Open our ears and hearts to your requests. Open our eyes to see the needs of others that can be helped by our efforts. Loosen our tongues to tell the world of the opportunities to be found in your service. Bless now the gifts we bring in Jesus' name. Amen.

COMMISSION AND BLESSING

Carry with you the mind of Christ,
   who emptied self to serve the Creator.
Equality with God is not for us to seek;
   our godlike pretensions are always misplaced.
Empty yourselves of all selfish ambition
   so you can hear the Sovereign's intentions.
As Christ took the humble role of a servant,
   we would focus first on ways to help others.
Being found in human form,
   Christ was obedient, even to death on a cross.
We sing the praises of our Savior,
   who heals our brokenness and affirms our worth.
God has exalted Jesus as the Christ
   and put the name of Jesus on every tongue.
Jesus Christ is our Sovereign,
   revealer of the One True God.
Amen. Amen.

Sixth Sunday of Lent
(Passion Sunday)

Old Testament: Isaiah 50:4–9a
                   Psalm 31:9–16
Epistle: Philippians 2:5–11
Gospel: Matthew 26:14—27:66 or 27:11–54

CALL TO WORSHIP

Come, people of God, to know again who you are,
   Return to the One who gives you life.
We come as children of God,
   longing for a closer walk with our Creator.
Morning by morning God wakens us to new possibilities
   and grants us the resources we need.

We have been given ears to hear, eyes to see,
 and tongues to share what we have been taught.
Jesus came among human beings as one of us,
 emptying himself in order to serve.
We would watch and pray with him,
 seeking to learn from his faithful witness.
Amen. Amen.

CALL TO CONFESSION

On this Passion Sunday we remember the intensity of suffering that marked Jesus' last hours on earth. As he upheld the banner of love, there was no one with enough courage to stand with him. The finger of betrayal, desertion, and denial points at all of us. Let us come to God as we are, recognizing how unworthy we are to approach the One who embraces the universe yet believing that we are known and welcomed in this Awesome Presence. Let us confess our sin.

PRAYER OF CONFESSION

O God, we do not want to suffer. We are not eager to relive the pain and agony Christ faced on our behalf or to identify with Christ's suffering at this difficult time. We prefer to avoid danger or, if the worst comes, to fight the battles our own way. We do not like to turn the other cheek and remain silent in the face of attack. We seek to justify ourselves, not empty ourselves. We try to save ourselves and shrink from helping to carry the cross. We want to wash our hands of all guilt and declare our innocence when some would accuse us of unfaithfulness. We cry, "My God, my God, why have you forsaken us?" when it is we who have done the forsaking. We cannot live with the burden of our sin. Grant us your forgiveness. In Christ's name. Amen.

ASSURANCE OF FORGIVENESS

Nothing can separate us from the love of God in Christ Jesus. We need not carry our burden of guilt for another moment. Trust God to supply all you need to live as a child of God. You are forgiven; you are loved; you are set free to respond with love to all you meet.

COLLECT

O Sovereign God, we have seen your love in the face of Christ; we have heard it in human words and experienced it in deeds of kindness and compassion. It is painful to remember the suffering of Jesus. Help us to learn from the stories of his last hours and to find strength for our own journeys through life. Let your face shine on your servants, and save us in your steadfast love. Amen.

OFFERTORY PRAYER

Thank you, God, for the greatest of all gifts, the saving action of Jesus Christ in human history. Your gift inspires our generous response. We

bring our offerings and renewed commitment. Help us to be faithful
disciples. Amen.

COMMISSION AND BLESSING

Go forth to serve, people of God.
  Live triumphantly through all temptation and suffering.
We are God's children, disciples of Jesus,
  eager to walk with Jesus during his holy week.
Go forth knowing that God is with you in all the
  possibilities of life.
Watch and pray with Jesus,
  learning from Christ's faithful witness.
When we are asked, "Friend, why are you here?"
  we will say, "To live and serve with Christ!"
God goes with you on your journey,
  loving, blessing, and upholding you.
Praise God for possibilities and opportunities to
  strengthen our faith and faithfulness. Amen.
Amen.

Monday of Holy Week

Old Testament: Isaiah 42:1–9
              Psalm 36:5–10
Epistle: Hebrews 9:11–15
Gospel: John 12:1–11

CALL TO WORSHIP

In Jesus Christ, God's chosen servant, our eyes are opened. Fresh winds
of the Spirit bring a new breath of life to all people. Come, expectantly
and fearlessly, to the mountaintops of God's love where righteousness
abounds. Feast on the abundance of God's grace. Drink from the streams
of living water. Walk with Christ through days of high anxiety and
powerful witness. Come, let us worship.

INVOCATION

Take us by the hand, God of all creation, so we will have the courage to
risk ourselves on behalf of your rule. In your light we see light and find
strength to make our witness. Your steadfast love sweeps across the
heavens and your faithfulness extends through the clouds. Recall us in
these moments to the covenant you have made with us, and equip us to
live within it. Amen.

CONFESSION OF SIN

In the shadow of God's wings
  we face ourselves as we really are.
We are afraid and shrink from danger;
  we rush to protect ourselves, before all else.
Before the One who did not cry out
  or break down under the rod,
We confess silences not born of strength
  or rooted in the courage of Christ.
In the presence of One who saw people's high intent
  and celebrated rather than judged,
We admit our tendency to point accusing fingers
  and measure people's worth by their possessions.
Before the embodiment of love and justice,
  who sided with the poor and oppressed,
We seek to mingle in high places
  and be recognized by the world's "great" ones.

ASSURANCE OF FORGIVENESS

God does not delight in a recital of our failures, but in a change of direction. God accepts us as we are and goes with us into a future filled with new possibilities. Let us accept our inheritance in Christ and the salvation promised to the upright of heart. Amen.

COLLECT

From graven images, O God, we turn to your truth and find our glory in no other. We long to feast on the abundance of your Word, through ancient texts that help to make you real to us. We are ready to listen. Help us to hear you speak. Amen.

OFFERTORY PRAYER

As Mary poured out expensive and prized ointment to anoint Jesus' feet, we would offer our best. Create in our midst worthy worship, uplifting programs, and loving service. We have feasted on your abundance, O God, and cannot keep it for ourselves. Bless our sharing, in Jesus' name. Amen.

COMMISSION AND BLESSING

We have been to this holy place with Christ;
  Now we go to declare the holiness of every place.
We have seen God's glory in worship.
  Now we go out to encounter God in every person.
You have peered into the heights and depths
  of God's glory and God's judgment.
We are prepared to share the vision
  and carry God's mercy to our sisters and brothers.

Go in peace and joy to serve where you are.
Christ goes with you and blesses you. Amen.
Amen.

Tuesday of Holy Week

Old Testament: Isaiah 49:1–7
Psalm 71:1–12
Epistle: 1 Corinthians 1:18–31
Gospel: John 12:20–36

INVOCATION

In you, O God, do we take refuge;
let us never be put to shame!
In your righteousness, deliver us and rescue us;
incline your ear to us and save us!
Be to us a rock of refuge,
a strong fortress to save us.
Rescue us, O God, from the hands of the wicked,
from the grasp of the unjust and the cruel.
For you, O God, are our hope;
upon you have we leaned from our birth.
Our mouths are filled with your praise
and with your glory all the day.
Do not cast us off in time of old age;
forsake us not when our strength is spent.
O God, be not far from us;
O God, make haste to help us!
Amen. **Amen.**

PRAYER OF CONFESSION

Eternal God, we have embraced the wisdom of this world as if knowledge could save us and our own cleverness could protect us. We have learned many secrets of the universe, only to turn them to destructive ends. We measure history by its wars and rally around those who carry big sticks. We have not dared to follow Jesus, who turned the other cheek and embraced the power of love. Forgive our misplaced loyalties and fear-filled priorities, as we seek to embrace a new faithfulness. Amen.

ASSURANCE OF FORGIVENESS

False wisdom is destroyed and wayward cleverness is thwarted. In God's economy, stumbling blocks and folly become channels of truth and power. The foolishness of God is wiser than human wisdom, and the weakness of God is stronger than human strength. You are freed from self-contempt and self-boasting to proclaim the goodness of God. Amen.

COLLECT

Great God, our Rock and Refuge, you named us in our mothers' bodies and called us from their wombs. We cannot escape your summons or cut ourselves off from the challenges of servanthood. We have been saved through the folly of preaching and the foolishness of the cross. We would see Jesus and die with him to all that is less than your plans for us. Grant us light and teach us to walk in it. Amen.

OFFERTORY PRAYER

With these offerings we scatter seeds that, by your grace, may take root, flourish, and bear much fruit. We would not spend our strength and your bounty for vanity. Lift us to the high purposes and firm resolve that marked the ministry of Christ, in whose name we dedicate ourselves with these gifts. Amen.

COMMISSION AND BLESSING

The call of God, in Christ Jesus,
   comes to weak, confused, unimportant people.
While the world calls for power and might,
   we hear a call to compassion and kindness.
The way of the cross is not an easy way,
   but it is the only path to life.
All who hoard and protect their lives lose them,
   and those who give their lives save them.
Do not be afraid to identify with Christ
   through the cruelty of this Holy Week.
We are ready to follow.
   May God guide us and inform our choices.
Amen. **Amen.**

Wednesday of Holy Week

Old Testament: Isaiah 50:4–9a
                    Psalm 70
Epistle: Hebrews 12:1–3
Gospel: John 13:21–30

CALL TO WORSHIP

As the cross looms ever closer and tensions mount inside us, we come to this time of worship with some weariness and fear. Jesus, the pioneer and perfecter of our faith, has faced shallow enthusiasm, prevailing indifferences, misguided disappointment, and fainthearted discipleship. The Savior announces calmly, "One of you will betray me," and we search our own souls lest we be the culprit. With heavy hearts we meet Christ here, to worship and adore.

INVOCATION

O Pioneer and Perfecter of the faith, you have run the race well, and we are panting and near exhaustion, far behind you. Awaken us to the possibilities you have in store for us. In life or in death we are your own. Meet us here and guide us. Amen.

CONFESSION OF SIN

Surrounded by a great cloud of witnesses,
    let us cast away the sin that clings so closely.
Be pleased to deliver us from our own folly,
    which we love to project on other people.
Behold, the Sovereign God helps us;
    who will declare us guilty?
We are betrayers who want to force Christ
    to do things another way—our way.
We have been hostile to God's Chosen One
    and called the way of Christ impractical.
We are not above selling out
    to protect our own advantages.
We go out into the night of our selfish pursuits
    when we could commune and be strengthened.
We are poor and needy, O God.
    Hasten to help us and deliver us.
Amen. **Amen.**

ASSURANCE OF FORGIVENESS

The evil in which we are enmeshed loses its power when we stay with Christ. With our Lord we can break away from false dependency and from rebellion and denial. Today is a new day. The past is forgiven. Awaken to God's good news! Amen.

COLLECT

We are ready to listen to the One who endured torture and death because he would not give up on us. Help us to face shame without feeling ashamed or striking back. Help us to bear hostility without becoming vindictive. Grant us the capacity to tolerate unfairness aimed at us but never to condone injustice that reflects badly on your church and causes innocent suffering. We await your word. Amen.

OFFERTORY PRAYER

For the joy that is set before us, we bring these gifts. With them we make haste to feed the hungry and house the homeless. Multiply our generosity with your own. Amen.

COMMISSION AND BLESSING
Scatter through God's world,
   surrounded by a great cloud of witnesses.
**We have laid aside every weight
   and every sin that clings so closely.**
Look to Jesus, the pioneer and perfecter
   of our faith.
**We are ready to endure and serve,
   following Jesus' example.**
The One who did not grow weary or fainthearted
   supplies all you need to serve faithfully.
**We are strengthened and empowered
   to be Christ's representatives.**
Amen. **Amen.**

Maundy Thursday

Old Testament: Exodus 12:1–14
                   Psalm 116:12–19
Epistle: 1 Corinthians 11:23–26
Gospel: John 13:1–15

CALL TO WORSHIP
Come, people of God, to know again who you are.
   Return to the One who gives you life.
**We come as children of God,
   longing for a closer walk with our Creator.**
This is the memorial observance of Jesus' last supper,
   a time for serious reflection and self-examination.
**We gather to break bread together
   and to experience our common life in the body of Christ.**
This is a time to put away divisions and grudges,
   to reach out with Christ's love to all sisters and brothers.
**As Jesus washed the feet of the disciples,
   we would humble ourselves in simple acts of kindness.**
The mandate of this holy night comes from Christ—
   "a new commandment . . . that you love one another."
**Even as Christ has loved us,
   we will enter wholeheartedly into love for all.**

CALL TO CONFESSION

We are welcome to come to Christ's banquet because of our own need. But we are also challenged to broaden our concern to include others—to identify with them in their difficulties, to feel with them the problems they face, to care about what happens to them, to be actively helpful. Unless our own needs are placed in this larger context, we cannot experience fully the forgiving love of God that Christ came to share with us. Let us come to God, recognizing how unworthy we are to approach the One who embraces the universe yet believing we are known and welcomed in this Awesome Presence. Let us confess our sin.

PRAYER OF CONFESSION

Eternal God, made known to us in Jesus of Nazareth, we come to this holy night recognizing that we share the self-centeredness, inattention, and fearfulness of the disciples. We are more concerned about our own place in life than we are about others' well-being. We say and do things that hurt others. We exaggerate or belittle our own gifts. We feel cut off from others, by our own action or theirs, by misunderstandings or deliberate intent. We have been more interested in saving face or getting even than in accepting the reconciling love Christ offers. We are reluctant to admit mistakes, ask forgiveness, or try new and better ways. Grant us courage to confess our limitations to one another as well as to you. Give us insight to understand ourselves, to face up to those attitudes and actions that have separated us from our best selves, from others, and from you. We want to learn to love as you have loved us. In Christ's name. Amen.

ASSURANCE OF FORGIVENESS

The apostle Paul wrote to church members in Corinth: "When we are judged by the Sovereign, we are chastened so that we may not be condemned along with the world." Times of self-examination and repentance are not to put us down, but to raise us up to new possibilities. This is a night for laying aside the burden of our fears, hatreds, and alienation, that God's love in Christ may reign in us. Forgiveness and renewal are God's gift to each of us; let us offer them to others. God loves you; accept that love and demonstrate it in your own life. Amen.

COLLECT

Prepare us, O God, to experience your Word as we hear again the Passover tradition of our Jewish ancestors in the faith and as we recall Jesus' last supper with a group of disciples. Equip us to enter once again into the covenant tradition of those who would take seriously the example of Christ. May our deeds of kindness and service be offered as an outpouring of your love for all of us. Amen.

OFFERTORY PRAYER

Thank you, God, for the privilege of entering fully into the body of
Christ. We are grateful for the opportunity to give ourselves and our
substance for the well-being of all humankind. We offer our lives in loving
service, our wealth in faithful stewardship, that the rule of God may be
acknowledged among all people. Amen.

COMMISSION AND BLESSING

You have been cleansed; you have communed;
   you are new creatures in Christ Jesus.
We have received God's forgiveness and blessing;
   we have been reconciled with our sisters and brothers.
Take with you the mandate we have from Christ:
   "Love one another, as I have loved you."
We will love in word and in deed,
   reaching out with helping hands and caring hearts.
Even in the face of rejection and suffering
   we can this night rejoice with Jesus the Christ.
We are free to make our witness to God's love
   without fear of the consequences.
You are the body of Christ and individually members of it;
   go forth to serve in Christ's name.
We face the world well equipped and unafraid.
   God, in Christ, goes with us every step of the way.
Amen. **Amen.**

Good Friday

Old Testament: Isaiah 52:13—53:12
                    Psalm 22:1–18
Epistle: Hebrews 4:14–16; 5:7–9
Gospel: John 18:1—19:42 or 19:17–30

CALL TO WORSHIP

Come, people of God, to know again who you are.
   Return to the One who gives you life.
We come as children of God,
   longing for a closer walk with our Creator.
Come to see and know the unique Child of God,
   who lived among us and died on our behalf.
Christ gave life itself to be a servant to all,
   but people despised and rejected the gift.
Christ was wounded for our transgressions
   and bruised for our iniquities.

**We believe Christ has borne our sins for us
and has sought and won our forgiveness.**
Let us draw near with true hearts,
in full assurance that our faith has meaning.
**Let us consider how to stir up one another
to live God's love and do good to all people.**

CALL TO CONFESSION

Today we remember one of the most tragic days in the world's history. A human being who embodied fully God's intention for all of us fell victim to the destructive power of evil. There were plausible reasons for those in authority to put him to death. In the name of public order and religious tradition they acted on behalf of what they determined to be the best interest of all people. Even his best friends did not dare to challenge this miscarriage of justice. As we put ourselves into this story, we are likely to be counted among either the oppressors or the cowardly friends. In either camp we have much to confess. Let us come to God, recognizing how unworthy we are to approach the One who embraces the universe, yet believing we are known and welcomed in this Awesome Presence. Let us confess our sin.

PRAYER OF CONFESSION

Sovereign God, we bow in grief that humankind could despise and reject your outpouring of love in Jesus Christ. How could we come to hold in jealous contempt One who embodied your intention for human life? "All we, like sheep, have gone astray; we have turned, every one of us, to our own way." We have hidden or denied our relationship with Christ when discipleship would be embarrassing or threatening. We have joined the oppressors when it seemed to our advantage to do so. At other times we have used our Christian identity as a claim to superiority; we have looked down on those who do not share our convictions. We are never far from violating your gospel of love. Once again, O God, we beg for forgiveness, believing that you have already turned the evil of this day to good. Amen.

ASSURANCE OF FORGIVENESS

"Christ bore the sins of many, and makes intercession for transgressors. Through suffering, Jesus learned obedience and became the source of eternal salvation to all who obey." We are forgiven; we are healed; we are new persons in Christ, who sets us free from our bondage to lesser gods that we might serve the One True God in joy and thanksgiving. Amen.

COLLECT

We who shrink from pain and suffering, open our minds and hearts to hear and feel the full impact of the evil day that has become Good Friday. Isaiah's suffering servant brings us face to face with the Christ of the Gospels. John's remembrances and interpretations help us to experience long-ago events. We are drawn to Jesus who proclaimed, "My realm is not of this world." May we acknowledge that rule even now in our midst. Amen.

OFFERTORY PRAYER

In the name of the One who gave life itself for us, we offer our tithes and offerings. May these gifts inspire further good works, following the example of Jesus Christ, in whose name we pray. Amen.

COMMISSION AND BLESSING

Who has believed what we have heard?
  And to whom has the arm of God been revealed?
We have witnessed the suffering of Christ for us;
  God's love for all people is clearly revealed.
God's servant was wounded for our transgressions
  and bruised for our iniquities.
We have seen and heard this truth;
  we have received healing and wholeness.
You are commissioned to tell the story,
  to share God's forgiving love with others.
We will stir up one another to love and good works,
  in faithful response to all we have received.
The blessing of Christ Jesus go with you
  through this day and into Easter's dawning. Amen.
Amen.

The Easter Season

Easter Sunday

Historic Message:	Acts 10:34–43
	Psalm 118:14–24
Epistle:	Colossians 3:1–11
Gospel:	John 20:1–18

CALL TO WORSHIP

This day is God's own creation!
We will rejoice and be glad in it!
Jesus Christ has broken the bonds of death!
We are witnesses to amazing good news!
Turn from your weeping and mourning.
Put aside the ways of death.
**We are being raised with Christ
to a new quality of life.**
The surprises of the resurrection
continue into our own day.
**The Risen Christ meets us here,
bringing us new life and hope.**

INVOCATION

Eternal God, we are caught up in the joy and promise of Easter. The healing ministry of Jesus cannot be put down or destroyed. The power of goodness and peace reigns over a broken world. We would cast away the anger, wrath, malice, and slander of our old nature that truth, righteousness, and love might dominate our thoughts and actions. May we hear, in this hour, the unmistakable accents of Jesus' presence with us. Free us to accept the good news Christ brings. Amen.

CALL TO CONFESSION

Easter brings a new day for all people. New life in Christ is offered, not just to a select chosen few, but to all who will respond in faith. Faith is not assenting to the unbelievable, but trusting an experience. The healing and transforming power of goodness and peace overpowers our anger and malice. The presence of Christ melts away our earthly deceits and invites us to a new authenticity. Let all that is evil within you be put to death this day, that the joy of Easter may truly be yours. Let us pour out before God all the sin and misery that separates us from the Holy One and from our own wholeness.

PRAYER OF CONFESSION

Holy God, we have propped up our lives with lies rather than devote ourselves to truth. We have allowed our thoughts to be polluted with selfish desires rather than focus on the well-being of all your people. We have coveted for ourselves the things of earth rather than aspire to the intentions of our Creator. We have embraced attitudes and actions that kill and destroy rather than those that build up and bring life and freedom. O God, we pray that you will break through all that divides and fragments us. We want to put off the old nature and put on the new. We want to be raised with Christ to a fresh quality of life. Make the resurrection a reality within and among us, we pray in Christ's name. Amen.

ASSURANCE OF FORGIVENESS

The apostle Peter proclaimed, "Every one who believes in Jesus Christ receives forgiveness of sins through this name." This is not a pious formula, but a reality all of us can experience. We are not bound by the forces of death or forever weighed down and oppressed by our own poor choices. Forgiveness is real. Today is a new day. Allow goodness and love a complete resurrection in your life.

COLLECT (PRAYER OF PREPARATION BEFORE THE SCRIPTURES)

Forgiving God, whose love shows no partiality, we seek to lay aside all the barriers that divide people from one another. We would accept for ourselves those values that are part of the new nature you intend for us. Turn our fear and uncertainty to a living faith. As we hear a story from the first Easter, grant us the joy of hearing Christ speak our names, welcoming us into discipleship. Amen.

OFFERTORY PRAYER

May our gifts give testimony to "the One ordained by God to be judge of the living and the dead." As we share in Christ's ministry of healing and reconciliation, pour out your spirit in our midst that we may be equipped and empowered to carry out your purposes. We cannot keep the good news to ourselves; teach us how to pass it on. Amen.

COMMISSION AND BLESSING

All who stand in awe before God
    and seek to do what God intends
    will know God's love in their lives.
We believe that good news is for us;
    a new day has dawned within us.
Go forth as witnesses to the living Christ,
    as persons who love and forgive in Jesus' name.
We are amazed that God forgives even our enemies
    and melts away the labels that keep us apart.

We are set free from our evil desires
and the contamination of our ugly passions.
We are being renewed day by day
in the image of our Creator.
The stone is rolled away;
Christ walks with us into this new week.
We will share good news
because it has become part of us.
Address the world with hope and joy.
We will greet our sisters and brothers
with love, joy, and peace.
Amen. **Amen.**

Easter Sunday (Alternate Reading)

Old Testament: Jeremiah 31:1–6
Psalm 118:14–24
Epistle: Acts 10:34–43
Gospel: Matthew 28:1–10

CALL TO WORSHIP
This is the day that God has made;
let us rejoice and be glad in it.
We celebrate good news: Jesus is risen!
We shall not die, but we shall live!
God is our strength and our song
and has become our salvation.
The stone which the builders rejected
has become the head of the corner.
Hear again the glad sounds of victory;
come and join the joyous dance of life.
We thank you, God, that you have answered our cries
and have become our salvation.
God's love is everlasting,
and God's faithfulness continues.
We have found grace in the wilderness of life
and are here to renew our promises in Christ.
Amen. **Amen.**

INVOCATION
Life-giving God, your promise of newness and rebirth is especially real to
us amid glad songs of victory, the fragrance of flowers, and the beauty of

today. Our senses are heightened, and we are able to feel your presence as we seldom know you in the dullness of our low expectations. Today we would dance with the merrymakers and loose our voices to sing hearty praise. We are witnesses to the resurrection. It is not just a long-ago event; it is today. Praise God! Amen.

COLLECT

How great is your name, O God, before whom we gather as equals in your sight. Whether we are first at the tomb or keep our distance, you care about us. In Christ you reach out to heal our brokenness and forgive our sins. Open our ears to the good news of Easter: we shall see the Risen One in all the places of our habitation, and the gift of the Holy Spirit will be ours. Amen.

OFFERTORY PRAYER

When our hopes lie buried, O God, your miracle occurs. Accomplish greater things than we could imagine with the substance we present in these moments. You plant vineyards and we enjoy the fruit. Enlist us now as co-laborers with Christ, wherever the summons to service may lead. Amen.

COMMISSION AND BLESSING

The stones are rolled away.
> The barriers to our faithfulness have been destroyed.

How good it is to renew our trust
> **and experience a rebirth of joy.**

Move beyond survival to fresh excitement.
> Our lives are changed by the Christ event.

We are part of a community of faith
> **on the move for Jesus Christ.**

God is building a new thing among us
> and invites us to celebrate, together and apart.

We go forth in the dance of the merrymakers,
> **for we have been renewed and empowered.**

Go with Christ through the Galilees of this week,
> that we may return again to share our stories.

Together we build the new story of Christ alive,
> **for we are Christ's body, in worship and service.**

Amen. **Amen.**

Second Sunday of Easter

Historic Message: Acts 2:14a, 22–32
                     Psalm 16:5–11
Epistle: 1 Peter 1:3–9
Gospel: John 20:19–31

CALL TO WORSHIP

Peace be with you, in the name of Jesus Christ,
  who has conquered death and shown us how to live.
We need the gift of peace for our harried days;
  and we need it for our troubled world.
God gives us counsel and instruction
  and is always available at our right hand.
Our hearts are glad and our souls rejoice;
  we shall not be moved.
In hope and confidence we come to praise God
  for the heritage and opportunity given to us.
We are full of gladness in the presence of Christ,
  whose ways we seek to follow.

INVOCATION

We come to you, O God, a believing but skeptical people. We have seen too much evil all around us, and within, to be convinced that Christ offers the last word. And yet we are drawn to the message and example Jesus lived among people like us. There is something genuine and compelling, in both word and deed, that we want to explore and affirm. Guide our inquiry and go with us in our struggle to understand and trust. In Jesus' name. Amen.

COLLECT

As we turn to the books written to evoke faith, we want to hear more than words. May we experience the presence of One whom death could not contain. Grant forgiveness and peace, and equip us to share these gifts. Amen.

OFFERTORY PRAYER

This offering is our most significant statement of faith, O God. We give because we believe this congregation is important, our ministry changes lives for the better, and we are part of something much larger than ourselves. Ultimately, we believe the church is our firmest link to your Reality. Use our time, talent, and treasure in ways that exceed our grandest design. Amen.

COMMISSION AND BLESSING

Go forth into the world in hope and peace,
  sharing the promise with all you meet.
We have been born anew to a living hope,
  in Christ, who is our peace.
Blessed are you when you learn to trust
  without all the proofs in place.
We have not seen and yet believe;
  Jesus Christ is God's special gift to the world.
Blessed are you when you forgive
  without knowing the offense will never be repeated.
We dare to forgive because God pardons us
  and summons us to be forgiving.
Blessed are you when you welcome the Holy Spirit,
  not knowing where God will lead.
We believe Christ sends us to continue the work
  started by Jesus of Nazareth long ago.
Peace be with you, in the name of Jesus Christ,
  who has conquered death and shown us how to live. Amen.
Amen.

Third Sunday of Easter

Historic Message:	Acts 2:14a, 36–41
(alternate)	Isaiah 43:1–12
	Psalm 116:12–19
Epistle:	1 Peter 1:17–23
Gospel:	Luke 24:13–35

CALL TO WORSHIP

L: Alleluia! Christ is risen!
P: The Lord is risen indeed. Alleluia!

L: Let the people assemble;
    God calls each one of us by name.
P: **The promises of God are to us and our children,**
    and to sisters and brothers near and far.
We gather as a community of faith,
    united in mutual concern and caring.
Here we break bread, learn, and pray together,
    and join in outreach to a needy world.
L: May our eyes and ears be open
    to the special message this hour holds for us.

P: **We will listen for God's living and abiding Word**
and strive to be obedient to the truth.
All: Amen. Amen.

INVOCATION

Loving God, who raised Jesus Christ from the dead to be our Savior, we are slow of heart to believe or accept our role as disciples. We are closer to the priests and rulers who wanted quiet, order, and business as usual. When you invite us to be born anew, we are not ready to take that risk. Yet we gather for this venture of worship, opening ourselves to your surprises. Meet us here and grant us courage to accept new possibilities for our lives. Amen.

COLLECT

We, whose eyes fail to see Christ among us and whose ears cannot discern your songs of love in our midst, come to your Word for renewed inspiration. Purify our souls that we may receive your salvation, truly love one another, and respond with glad and generous hearts. Amen.

OFFERTORY PRAYER

In the name of Christ, whose blood was poured out to ransom and redeem us, we bring these tokens of our intent to share. We may not be ready for significant sacrifice or to sell our possessions and divide the proceeds as people have need. However, we do want to be generous with our gifts and our time. We are glad for the opportunity to give. Amen.

COMMISSION AND BLESSING

The Sovereign Christ go with you, as you depart
to witness to your faith and hope in God.
Our hearts burned within us as we recognized
the presence of Christ in our worship.
Be alert to use your eyes and ears well this week,
lest you fail to see and hear what God has in store.
We do not want to miss a vision of angels
or the profound encounter of table fellowship.
Love one another earnestly, from the heart;
enjoy opportunities to give what others need.
May our deeds be consistent with our profession
of Jesus Christ as our Sovereign and Guide.
Receive the gift of the Holy Spirit,
that you may be saved from this crooked generation.
God gives us confidence to face life anew,
with greater sensitivity and awareness.
Amen. Amen.

Fourth Sunday of Easter

Historic Message: Acts 2:42–47
                                  Psalm 23
Epistle: 1 Peter 2:19–25
Gospel: John 10:1–10

CALL TO WORSHIP

Our shepherd invites us to this time of worship;
    our God leads us by refreshing waters.
As we share our lives with one another
    our souls are restored.
God leads us in paths of righteousness
    and adds to our company day by day.
We would devote ourselves to the gospel
    and remember one another in our prayers.
God supplies our daily bread
    for both body and soul.
We will partake of physical and spiritual food
    with glad and generous hearts.
Remember the One in whose name we worship,
    Jesus Christ, who died amidst the world's suffering.
Christ came that all might have an abundant life;
    we acknowledge and rejoice in this gift.
Amen. **Amen.**

INVOCATION

Lead us now, O God, through the maze of our existence, as you led your people long ago. Keep us from resisting your word of judgment or shrinking from the challenges of discipleship. Call us by name and show us the pathways you would have us travel. In Jesus' name. Amen.

COLLECT

O Great Shepherd, whose presence was discerned in the history of our spiritual forebears, we come to you, a fearful people who resist the Holy Spirit and shrink from undeserved suffering. We want to trust your promise of abundant life. Speak to us that we may seek, above all else, to do what is pleasing to you. Amen.

OFFERTORY PRAYER

Remembering Jesus Christ, who bore our sins, we bring these tokens of our gratitude. We would die to sin and live righteously, in thanksgiving for Christ's sacrifice for us. May we as a church of generous and joyful

people use these offerings in ways that reflect renewed discipleship.
Amen.

COMMISSION AND BLESSING
    In growing obedience to the One whom faith reveals,
        take your part in the ministry of Christ Jesus.
    We join with the whole church in prayer,
        attention to the Word, and acts of charity.
    Listen for the prompting of the Holy Spirit,
        who offers you wisdom and understanding.
    We rejoice in God's gift of the law,
        praying for insight and courage to live by it.
    May the Spirit grant you life so abundant
        that you will experience new energy for every task.
    In covenant with the Creator of all worlds,
        we devote ourselves to the best interests
        of all people in this world, in Jesus' name.
    Amen. **Amen.**

Fifth Sunday of Easter

Historic Message: Acts 7:55–60
                       Psalm 31:1–8
Epistle: 1 Peter 2:2–10
Gospel: John 14:1–14

CALL TO WORSHIP
    Let us come away from our regular routines,
        our limited perceptions, our counterfeit piety.
    We come eagerly, with high expectations,
        to wrestle with scriptures and their implications.
    Seek what is genuine, lasting, and helpful,
        putting away insincerity, malice, and guile.
    We seek refuge from our detractors
        and delivery from idols and shame.
    May we commit our ways to the Sovereign's hand,
        as we rejoice in God's steadfast love.
    God is our rock and our fortress,
        leading and guiding us day by day.
    We are chosen and precious, God's own people,
        destined to lead others to God's marvelous light.

Jesus Christ, the cornerstone of our faith,
   invites us to be part of God's spiritual household.
Amen. **Amen.**

INVOCATION

Merciful God, we join in worship in the assurance that there is a place for us in your plans. We ask for discernment to recognize our special gifts and courage to use them. Quiet people's opposition to the good news so they will recognize that we are not turning the world upside down, but helping to turn it right side up, for the sake of all. Keep our worship focused on your action, in Christ, on our behalf; we pray in Jesus' name. Amen.

COLLECT

Feed us, O God, with the pure spiritual milk that will nourish us and equip us to follow the One who is the way, the truth, and the life. May we not only declare your wonderful deeds, but also undertake the "greater works" to which Christ summoned all who would follow as disciples of the Most High. Amen.

OFFERTORY PRAYER

We have tasted your kindness, O God, and want to share it with others. We have witnessed your saving grace in Jesus Christ, and give thanks for all your care. We have heard the call to even "greater works," and here dedicate our offerings and ourselves to that end. Amen.

COMMISSION AND BLESSING

Declare the wonderful deeds of God,
   who brought you from night to day.
God has built us into a spiritual house
   with Jesus Christ as the chief cornerstone.
Do not lose heart or be jealous of others;
   rather, taste the kindness of God and rejoice.
We will not despair if our work and witness
   are opposed and rejected.
God, in Christ, declares there is a place for you;
   in loving mercy you are chosen by God.
We will seek to honor Christ in all circumstances,
   for Christ is the way, the truth, and the life.
Ask, and God will provide all you need;
   believe, and your works will proclaim God's glory.
May God help us to know when to be bold
   and when to make our quiet witness.
Amen. **Amen.**

Sixth Sunday of Easter

Historic Message: Acts 17:22–31
  Psalm 66:8–20
Epistle: 1 Peter 3:13–22
Gospel: John 14:15–21

CALL TO WORSHIP

Come to the source of all truth,
  to the author of life.
We dare to approach our Creator
  in humility and thanksgiving.
God calls us away from worship of things,
  from idols that block our view of God.
God is unknown to us
  only when we have shut off the contact.
In Christ, God comes to us again, saying,
  "I will not leave you desolate."
We need the Counselor who will listen to us,
  who will hear our evil and not turn away.
Let us open our lives to the Spirit of Truth,
  as we seek new life in Christ.

INVOCATION

Loving God, in whom we live and move and have our being, dwell with us here, transforming the landscape of our souls and granting the nourishment we need. We are hungry for your truth and thirsty for real peace. Hear our prayer and praise. Turn us away from evil. Prepare us for life. Amen.

COLLECT

We come to your Word, O God, not as a pious religious act, but to prepare ourselves to live fully, as you intend. We want to witness to our faith with honest speech and loving deeds. Teach us reverence, gentleness, and faithfulness. Amen.

OFFERTORY PRAYER

Eternal God, beyond the limitations of silver and gold, we bring to your altar what is valuable to us, that you may bless and multiply our efforts to make faithful response. We would send our best for the sake of the poor and the needy, recognizing that we also have need of what others can share with us. We depend on your love, received day by day and passed on by each of us to all who journey through life together. Thank you for all your gifts. Amen.

COMMISSION AND BLESSING

Go forth, with gentleness and reverence,
to proclaim the hope that is in you.
We have sensed Mystery no words can explain,
reality that transcends our human limitations.
All who love life and long to see good days,
keep your tongues from evil deception.
The Spirit of Truth has come to us;
we would keep faith with the God who loves us.
You are called to seek peace, to pursue it,
to turn evil away with deeds of kindness.
God's love for all humankind unites us
as one family and one nation on this planet.
Do not shrink from sacrifice and suffering
when your cause is right and just.
Without arrogant pretension, we work for justice
and give ourselves away that others may live.
Amen. **Amen.**

Ascension

Historic Message: Acts 1:1–11
Psalm 47
Epistle: Ephesians 1:15–23
Gospel: Luke 24:46–53 or Mark 16:9–16, 19–20

CALL TO WORSHIP

5/19/96

Our human scene has been caressed
by a visit from the Eternal.
God's realm has broken into our history
and revised all our possibilities.
Clap, shout, and sing praises.
God reigns over all the earth.
The Risen One has become head of all things
and we are moved, as disciples, to worship.
This is a time to bless God and rejoice
in the fulfillment of law, prophets, and psalms.
We join the innumerable company of the saints
in praise, thanksgiving, and witness.
Amen. **Amen.**

INVOCATION

Almighty God, we are seldom moved by the sound of great words or visions of fire and clouds. Our doubts are often more compelling than our faith. Yet you break through our reservations and protective devices to baptize us with the Holy Spirit, and we cannot miss the joy. In this hour we would look up to know you and then go out to serve all whom you love. In Jesus' name. Amen.

COLLECT

Lift us to your Holy Presence, God of all worlds, that we may touch reality beyond human knowing and partake of the inheritance you have promised us. Pour your spirit upon us, that we may live with hope and fulfill Christ's commission to make disciples of all nations. Amen.

OFFERTORY PRAYER

Clothe us with power, O God, that our offerings and our lives may make a compelling witness to your love for all the saints. Enlighten our hearts that we may share with all the hope to which we have been called. Keep us faithful to the tasks you set before your church. Amen.

COMMISSION AND BLESSING

The Human One has lived among us
and lifted our spirits to the mountaintops.
Because we have seen the Eternal in Jesus Christ,
God has been made real to us.
We celebrate the reign of the Human One
over all the realms of heaven and earth.
God has raised our Savior
to dominion, glory, and sovereignty.
Now God calls us to be the church, Christ's body,
witnessing to the ends of the earth.
We extend love and forgiveness in Christ's name
and seek to make disciples to all nations.
Amen. **Amen.**

Seventh Sunday of Easter

Historic Message: Acts 1:6–14
                     Psalm 68:1–10
Epistle: 1 Peter 4:12–14; 5:6–11
Gospel: John 17:1–11

CALL TO WORSHIP

We do not know the time or season
of God's visitation among us.
But we await God's promise
as we gather in this house of prayer.
Cast all your anxieties on God,
for God cares about you.
We long for support and comfort
and for assurance of eternal life.
God will establish and strengthen you;
rejoice as you share Christ's suffering.
We humble ourselves under God's mighty hand
and are watchful, as we stand firm in faith.
Christ intercedes for all disciples,
that we may know God's love and care.
We join Christ in prayer that we may all be one,
as Christ is one with the Creator.
Amen. **Amen.**

CALL TO CONFESSION

Unrepeatable moments are offered to us—times to make choices, to decide for or against discipleship. Sometimes we stand staring into the heavens without any expectation of a response. Sometimes we go through the motions of worship but close our hearts to avoid encounter with the living God. We are invited to open our inner being to know and be known, in these moments of confession.

PRAYER OF CONFESSION

Your judgment begins with us, O God, for we have chosen to identify ourselves as Christians. Yet we have wandered from your ways, dealt treacherously with others, broken your law, and violated the purity of word and spirit that you expect of your people. Forgive us, Holy God, for the sake of Jesus Christ, whom we intend to follow, with renewed commitment. Amen.

ASSURANCE OF FORGIVENESS

God gathers the wanderers and restores those in captivity and exile to the household of faith. God's mercy extends to all who resist wrong and seek to do what is right. Dwell in God's presence in confidence and trust; there none can make you afraid.

COLLECT

May your word draw us together, cause us to look up, and then send us forth to do the truth we have heard. We are not ashamed to live simply, to forego the world's perception of success, or even to suffer for the faith you entrust to us. Teach us to pray for others as Christ prayed for us. Amen.

OFFERTORY PRAYER

May the work of Christ be accomplished through these gifts and through our faithful attention to the tasks you call us to do. Amen.

COMMISSION AND BLESSING

Christ sends you into the world
to be channels of God's visitation.
We carry the Spirit of prayer from this place,
opening ourselves to God's promises.
Minister to all who are torn by fear or failure,
and feel the pain of all who suffer.
We will share our faith in a God who cares
and cling with our peers to Eternal Hope.
Take your share of suffering
as a witness to God's love in Christ.
We entrust ourselves to our faithful Creator,
finding cause for rejoicing even when reviled.
Christ prays for our unity
and empowers our witness.
We will follow where Christ leads
and claim our oneness with all whom Christ loves.
Amen. Amen.

The Pentecost Season

Pentecost Sunday

Old Testament: Isaiah 44:1–8
Psalm 104:24–34
Epistle: Acts 2:1–21
1 Corinthians 12:3b–13
Gospel: John 20:19–23 or 7:37–39

CALL TO WORSHIP
God promised through a prophet long ago:
I will pour out my spirit on all flesh.
Our sons and daughters shall prophesy,
the young see visions, and the old dream dreams.
God's spirit opens minds and hearts
to make the commonplace exceptional.
We want to see, hear, and feel
what the Holy Spirit has in store for us.
Listen for the wind and feel the flames;
be alert for God's surprises.
Come, Holy Spirit, to make all things new;
light the flame of love in our lives.
Amen. Amen.

CALL TO CONFESSION
The great and terrible day of God was, to the Old Testament prophet Joel,
a time of judgment. He envisioned blood, smoke, and darkness. But from
the depths of destruction and death there emerged, for both Joel and
Peter, the New Testament apostle, possibilities for salvation. When threat
and change are upon us, we are most ready to see God's signs and accept
new opportunities. Ready or not, the Holy Spirit comes, and we are
invited to put into words how things are going in our lives. Let us make
our confession to Almighty God.

PRAYER OF CONFESSION
Amazing God, we are bewildered by our continuing inability to make
sense out of life. Our visions and dreams far outpace reality, and our
expectations of ourselves are seldom realized. We do not do the good we
intend, and the evil we thought we had left behind comes back to haunt
us. In our relations with others there seems to be no common language to
unite us, and we resist including everyone in our concerns. Forgive our
sluggish responses and our resistance to change. Purify and enliven us by
your Spirit at work within and among us. Amen.

78

ASSURANCE OF FORGIVENESS

Receive the Holy Spirit. Our alienation·from God is ended. God takes us beyond our quarrels with sisters and brothers. We can live at peace with ourselves. The Sovereign One, on whose name we have called, has acted to save us. Accept the good news of forgiveness and pass on the gift. "If you forgive the sins of any, they are forgiven; if you retain the sins of any, they are retained." Praise God with your whole being! Amen.

COLLECT (PRAYER OF PREPARATION BEFORE THE SCRIPTURES)

You are the first and the last; there is none beside you. How manifold are your works! Confront us, Holy God, with wind and fire that transform life. We are amazed at what we do not understand and tempted to dismiss wonders beyond our experience. Break through our reserve to set us free. As we listen with expectancy, grant us courage to accept the challenges Christ presents to us. Amen.

OFFERTORY PRAYER

On the first day of the week we bring the first fruits of all our efforts for your blessing. We want our offerings to empower today's disciples, as the mighty wind and tongues of fire inspired and equipped the early apostles. As they gave their all to build your church, we rededicate our lives to making the church a vital force in today's world. Amen.

COMMISSION AND BLESSING

The fire is burning in your life;
    don't let it go out.
God has set us ablaze with new possibilities,
    and we are excited about where God may lead.
You have a message to share;
    don't mute or silence it.
The wind blows where it will,
    and we will not seek to divert it.
As God sent Jesus into the world,
    so Christ sends us to make a difference.
We will go where Christ leads
    and be alert to God's continuing surprises.
Sing to the Holy One as long as you live;
    praise God with your whole being.
We will declare God's creative power to all
    and speak of the manifold works of the Spirit.
Amen. **Amen.**

Trinity Sunday

Old Testament: Deuteronomy 4:32–40
Psalm 33:1–12
Epistle: 2 Corinthians 13:5–14
Gospel: Matthew 28:16–20

CALL TO WORSHIP

God's Spirit is moving through our gathering,
    creating and recreating, judging and empowering.
Let God's light break forth to illumine us
    and the shadows be dispelled.
The earth brings forth life-giving food,
    and our need for nourishment is supplied.
We give thanks for the sustenance God provides
    and seek to share it with all humankind.
God grants us dominion over the planet's resources
    and calls us to be stewards of the earth.
We seek insight and willpower
    to use God's gifts with prudence and imagination.
God pronounces all creation good
    and joins us for a day of renewal.
We rejoice in our sabbath opportunities
    as we celebrate this resurrection day.

CALL TO CONFESSION

We are invited to examine ourselves, to see whether we are holding to our faith. Is Christ alive in us? Are we living the truth? Let us give public testimony to the state of our faith, as we confess our sin.

PRAYER OF CONFESSION

Triune God, we acknowledge you as our Creator, Redeemer, and Sustainer. You grant us opportunities to be co-creators, but we cling to our ruts and routines. You expand the horizons of our caring, only to have our prejudices and selfishness intrude on your generosity in Christ. You send your Spirit to empower us, and we waste the power you supply in meaningless activity. Awaken us from our apathy, forgive our laziness, and rechannel our priorities, we pray in Jesus' name. Amen.

ASSURANCE OF FORGIVENESS

God promises to be with us, to redirect our ways, to grant us peace. We are forgiven. We are loved. We are united with one another. We are strengthened to mend our ways. May the God of love and peace abide with us. Amen.

COLLECT

Creator of all worlds, who has made us in your own image, help us to see your goodness in all things and in all people. May confidence that you live in us develop our capacity to listen to one another, live in peace, and welcome opportunities to minister in your world. Amen.

OFFERTORY PRAYER

You created a universe and entrusted this planet to us, Great God. We have received life and abilities from your hand and return these offerings to further your reign among us. Only you know how adequately we are responding. May what we dedicate here, and the cause that engages our attention, represent an improvement in our stewardship. Amen.

COMMISSION AND BLESSING

God's Spirit sends us into the world
    to live creatively and faithfully.
We will walk in the light
    and celebrate the goodness of God.
Be faithful in your stewardship
    and fruitful in your teaching.
We heed Christ's call to make disciples
    in all lands, among all peoples.
Discover and build on agreements among you,
    and find ways to promote true peace.
We commit ourselves anew to live as
    truth-seekers and peacemakers.
The grace of Jesus Christ
    and the love of God
    and the communion of the Holy Spirit
    be with you all. Amen.
Amen.

Second Sunday After Pentecost

Old Testament: Genesis 12:1–9
              Psalm 33:18–22
Epistle: Romans 3:21–28
Gospel: Matthew 7:15–29

CALL TO WORSHIP

As a faith community, and as individuals,
    we address God, our Father and Mother:

O Sovereign, our Sovereign,
   you alone would we worship.
Every sound tree bears good fruit;
   we are known by our fruit.
Our church has done mighty works in Christ's name
   and each of us has sought to be loyal.
The fruit of the Spirit is love, joy, and peace,
   patience, kindness, goodness,
   faithfulness, gentleness, and self-control,
We have no grounds for boasting
   but are justified by faith, apart from the law.
Let us seek God's mercy
   and be led by God's Spirit.
We bow before the Most High
   to find acceptance and instruction.
Amen. Amen.

CALL TO CONFESSION

Jesus cautioned "followers of the way" to beware of false prophets and to judge carefully according to fruits of faith that could be observed. Not everyone who claims loyalty to God shall enter the realm of heaven. They may hear instead, "Depart from me, you evildoers." We come to God now to confess, as honestly as we can, how good and evil, faith and doubt, mingle in us.

PRAYER OF CONFESSION

Gracious God, we have sinned and fallen short of your glory. Your word is not last on our lips at night or first in our thoughts at dawn. We have failed to instill your way in our children or seek your will in our daily conversations and decision-making. We have turned aside to pursue other gods, and the truth is not in us. Again, we throw ourselves on your mercy, begging for forgiveness and a fresh start, in Jesus' name. Amen.

ASSURANCE OF FORGIVENESS

In divine forbearance God has passed over your former sins. If you obey the commandments of your God, a blessing is promised. Therefore, write God's Word in your heart and soul, and turn joyously to God's assurance throughout your days. You are blessed so you can be a blessing to others. Amen.

COLLECT

Righteous God, so fill us with your steadfast love that our hearts and souls are surrounded daily with your truth. Help us to build on strong foundations. Nurture our faith so we may bear good fruit, by the authority and power of Jesus Christ. Amen.

OFFERTORY PRAYER

Your grace, O God, is a gift that nothing can match. The greatest offering
we can make is to live according to your will. Grant wings to these gifts,
that they may soar to do your bidding. Bring a melody to our lips, that our
days may be songs of praise. In Christ's service. Amen.

COMMISSION AND BLESSING

Build wisely on the solid rock of faith
    that wind and rain cannot destroy.
Our trust is in God, beyond our knowing
    but revealed in the law and the prophets.
God promises to be with you, to bless you,
    and make you a blessing to others.
We will keep God's word in our hearts
    and share it with all who learn from us.
Bear fruit befitting your commitment;
    live in love, joy, and peace.
God grant us patience, kindness, goodness,
    faithfulness, gentleness, and self-control.
The blessing of the Sovereign One your God
    be upon you and remain with you. Amen.
Amen.

Third Sunday After Pentecost

Old Testament: Genesis 22:1–18
                     Psalm 13
Epistle: Romans 4:13–25
Gospel: Matthew 9:9–13

CALL TO WORSHIP

As surely as the new day has dawned,
    God comes to meet us and be known by us.
I will sing to God and trust God's steadfast love.
    My heart rejoices in God's saving grace.
God gives life to the dead
    and creates new things from nothing.
We believe, against all hope,
    that new life can be wrought in us.
Jesus invited people to fresh starts
    with the words "Follow me."
We want to respond with our lives,

to take the risks of discipleship.
God will raise us up and equip us
  for our life of service.
We rejoice in God's promises
  and devote this hour to prayer and praise.
Amen. **Amen.**

CALL TO CONFESSION

We need not fear to approach God with all the blots and stains that make us unattractive and destroy our self-confidence. God welcomes honest confession and frees us from our slavery to sin. Let us come boldly to the throne of grace to find acceptance and help.

PRAYER OF CONFESSION

Merciful God, we have been quick to criticize and slow to offer our devotion. Our love is as fleeting as the dew, and just as fragile, before every hint of disapproval. We have relied on rituals rather than on righteousness, knowing about Jesus rather than taking our rightful role in the body of Christ. We have used others for our own ends and shrunk from offering our resources to them. Forgive our self-centeredness and engage us in ministry, we pray. Amen.

ASSURANCE OF FORGIVENESS

We are welcomed into God's presence by forgiving love that will not let us go. Christ came to call sinners to repentance. The Great Physician ministers to the sick and hurting ones, including us. Rejoice and give glory to God, as you grow in faith and love. Amen.

COLLECT

We who are forgiven sinners turn to you, O God, for healing and comfort. Grant us grace to hear the promise of faith, hope, and love spoken to people of former times and shared again to meet our own need. We seek the courage to trust you and follow Christ, wherever that may lead us. Amen.

OFFERTORY PRAYER

We bring our offerings to the table of Christ, not as taxes to be paid, or as sacrifices to be blessed, but as an outpouring of love. We have known acceptance and healing, forgiveness and grace. All that is dearest to us we give in gratitude for all we have received. Amen.

COMMISSION AND BLESSING

Let us press on to know the Eternal One,
  who desires our steadfast love.
Day by day we will live by faith
  and trust the promises of God.
Our faith in God, who raised Jesus from death,

is reckoned to us as righteousness.
We are justified by faith,
 not by religious acts or works of the law.
Christ came not to call the righteous, but sinners,
 to heal the sick, not the satisfied.
Aware of our need and eager to find life
 we answer Christ's call, "Follow me."
The grace of Jesus Christ
 and the love of God
 and the communion of the Holy Spirit
 be with you today and forever. Amen.
Amen.

Fourth Sunday After Pentecost

Old Testament: Genesis 25:19–34
 Psalm 46
Epistle: Romans 5:6–11
Gospel: Matthew 9:35—10:15

CALL TO WORSHIP
Come, behold the works of the Living God!
 Listen for what God would say to us.
We await God's word for our church
 and for the times in which we live.
God beckons us to remember
 the support and promptings of the Spirit.
We have received comfort and assurance,
 and our eyes have been opened to God's challenges.
God does not let us escape the world's pain
 when we come to this place apart.
Some of the pain is our own, and we seek relief.
 Much is borne by others, whom we want to help.
God is our refuge and strength,
 a very present help in trouble.
We open ourselves to God's healing
 and offer ourselves for further service.
Amen. **Amen.**

CALL TO CONFESSION
Come to the One who justifies and reconciles, who knows us as we are

and yet reaches out to draw us into the realm of God. Be still and know that God is God. Let us confess our sin.

PRAYER OF CONFESSION
Powerful and Merciful God, you have blessed us abundantly, and we have complained. You have linked our lives with others, and we have abused their trust. We have despised our birthright and misused your blessing. We have left undone many of the tasks you set before us, while pursuing passions and pleasures that have become our gods. We have strayed so far from the truth that we find truth hard to recognize. We are sinners with no place to turn except to your compassion and salvation, pleading for forgiveness and strength to lead a new life in Christ Jesus. Amen.

ASSURANCE OF FORGIVENESS
While we were yet sinners, Christ died for us. In our weakness God offers Christ's strength. In our alienation from God, Christ is the reconciler who draws us back to eternal verities. The life of Christ invites us into the stream of salvation, where healing waters flow. Our thirst is quenched and there is plenty of water to share. God equips us, as forgiven sinners, to labor in fields ripe for harvest. Praise God!

COLLECT
Ruler and Lover of the earth and all humankind, we would hear the good news from your realm, where the sick are healed and the dead are raised to new life. We would obey your voice, live in covenant with you, and offer your peace to a needy world. Show us our rightful place in the fields ready for your harvest. Amen.

OFFERTORY PRAYER
Eternal God, we have heard Jesus direct us to travel light through life, but many prized possessions weigh us down. We enjoy them! At your altar we are faced with hard choices. Dedication of these offerings is but a prelude to further struggle. How shall we deploy all the resources you entrust to our care? Amen.

COMMISSION AND BLESSING
As Jesus sent out the first disciples,
the church scatters us for service.
We see the needs and they scare us;
surely others could be more helpful.
Jesus chose ordinary people as apostles,
tapping abilities they did not know they had.
How can we slow people down enough to listen?
And where is there time for spiritual matters?
The twelve identified with people in their need,
those who were sick, outcasts, or confused.

Our listening may release healing possibilities,
   and our prayers open us to God's power within us.
The realm of heaven is at hand.
   God gives us authority to transform life now.
We are ready to offer God's peace to our world
   and give ourselves that others may know peace.
Amen. **Amen.**

Fifth Sunday After Pentecost

Old Testament: Genesis 28:10–17
                  Psalm 91:1–10
Epistle: Romans 5:12–19
Gospel: Matthew 10:16–33

CALL TO WORSHIP

Come together, disciples of Jesus,
   who dwell in the shadow of the Most High.
God is our refuge and fortress.
   We will not fear daytime threats or nighttime terror.
God promises to keep you wherever you go.
   There is nowhere you can go that God is not.
Surely God is in this place;
   this is the house of God and the gate of heaven.
God continues to value your uniqueness
   and sends salvation for your patient endurance.
We have known God's grace as a free gift;
   God's love surrounds us and supports us.
Let Christ be your teacher and example
   and the Holy Spirit, your inspiration and guide.
When God calls we will answer;
   with our whole lives we will serve our God.

CALL TO CONFESSION

All of us share in the sin of humankind that separates us from God, others,
and our own best selves. We also have available to us the free gift of God's
grace. Let us once again seek that gift as we remember and renounce our
failure.

PRAYER OF CONFESSION

O God, we are afraid our wrongdoing will be discovered and avenged. We
fear the deep recesses of our own evil and anger, and we project them on

The Pentecost Season   87

the world around us. Sometimes our pride gets in the way of growth. Perhaps we have wanted to be greater than our teacher, to avoid the taunts and betrayal Jesus endured. Forgive us, God, for being so wrapped up in ourselves that we can see neither our sin nor the way you value us. Keep us from denying you in word or deed, and grant us your salvation. Amen.

ASSURANCE OF FORGIVENESS

By the obedience of one, Jesus Christ, you have been counted righteous. Your prayers have reached God. You have been delivered from death to life. Grace abounds. Those who seem powerfully arrayed against you cannot kill your soul. Why, even the hairs of your head are numbered. Therefore, trust God and do not be anxious.

COLLECT

O God, whose ways we do not understand, we bring our anxiety and resentment to this time of seeking your Word through the holy scriptures. There is unfairness all around and terror in the night. We hesitate to speak up for what we believe. We fear one another and are frightened by your judgment. Break through our limited perceptions. Reassure us and help us to believe in ourselves and in you. Amen.

OFFERTORY PRAYER

Sometimes it is hard to see results from the gifts we share. Evil continues to thrive. Needs multiply. What have we accomplished with all our efforts? Yet our faith will not be put out, and hope abounds. We do not know what to say. But we believe that we are heard, that you care, and that what we are giving, by your grace, is making a difference somewhere. In humility we dedicate these gifts and renew our commitment to your purposes. Amen.

COMMISSION AND BLESSING

We are sent out as sheep in the midst of wolves,
    but God is with us and evil cannot overcome us.
We want to face evil with quiet confidence
    that nothing can separate us from a loving God.
Do not be anxious about what you will say or do,
    for the Spirit will speak and act through you.
As disciples, we are God's instruments,
    channels for God's grace.
Let us proclaim from the housetops
    the love we have seen in Jesus Christ:
Christ, our Savior and Example, pleads our case
    before our Mother and Father in heaven.
Do not grow weary in well-doing.
    A disciple should be like the teacher.

In waking and dreaming, God adds to our understanding
and enables us to witness to God's truth.
Amen. Amen.

Sixth Sunday After Pentecost

Old Testament: Genesis 32:22–32
                    Psalm 17:1–7, 15
Epistle: Romans 6:1–11
Gospel: Matthew 10:34–42

CALL TO WORSHIP

Come before God as a family of Christ's people,
  in whom our Risen Sovereign lives and serves.
**It is an awesome thing that God's Chosen One
  continues to minister through us.**
How blessed you are when you reach out
  to do more than the expected.
**It is a joy to offer hospitality
  and provide what others need most.**
Those who give support to the righteous
  shall receive the reward of a righteous person.
**The links forged by our faith call forth loyalty
  that even our families cannot command.**
All who risk themselves for Christ's sake
  will find abundant life through the cross.
**Whether a cross or a cup of cold water is required,
  we want to give ourselves to the tasks at hand.**
Amen. Amen.

CALL TO CONFESSION

People who live closest to God are most aware of their shortcomings and
need for forgiveness. Saints, more than grievous offenders against God
and humanity, are convinced that growth and reconciliation are neces-
sary. All of us know some gaps in our lives between the way things are and
how they should be. In humility and expectation let us come to God in
prayer.

PRAYER OF CONFESSION

Uncreated God, above all the gods we create, we are not eager to take up
a cross to follow Jesus. We would rather help out in safe places where we
can protect those persons and things most dear to us. We shrink from the

difficult choices that may separate us from loved ones with differing views. We even have some favorite sins we would like to continue. But we know that life for us is not all it is meant to be. We long for true reconciliation with your purposes for us. Forgive us, we pray, that we might die to sin and rise to new life in Christ, in whose name we pray. Amen.

ASSURANCE OF FORGIVENESS
Your old self was crucified with Christ, according to the scriptures. You are no longer enslaved to sin. Walk, therefore, in newness of life. Amen.

COLLECT
Glorious God, our Mother and Father, guide us to put first things first in our lives. May our priorities always center in your purposes for us. We, who have been baptized into Jesus Christ, seek to fulfill our discipleship in all our thoughts, words, and deeds. Amen.

OFFERTORY PRAYER
What shall we offer as a fitting response to your abounding grace? Will our offerings support a prophet's ministry in our midst and to the world? Will they extend a cup of pure water in a thirsty land and life-sustaining food when there has been no hope? Will they ennoble us for more creative outreach? Bless our gifts with affirmative answers in which we can rejoice. In Jesus' name. Amen.

COMMISSION AND BLESSING
As you depart to serve, be aware of people
   who are depending on your best efforts.
God's work is accomplished through and in spite of
   our commitment to a faithful witness.
God surprises us with unexpected rewards
   at those times we are most selfless in our giving.
The opportunity to be truly helpful to others
   is its own reward.
Take up your cross;
   it is a symbol of life, not death.
We take risks for Christ's sake,
   knowing that it is the only way we will find life.
The grace of Christ, love of God,
   and communion of the Holy Spirit
   abide with you and equip you for every good work. Amen.
Amen.

Seventh Sunday After Pentecost

Old Testament: Exodus 1:6–14, 22—2:10
                    Psalm 124
Epistle: Romans 7:14–25a
Gospel: Matthew 11:25–30

CALL TO WORSHIP

Hear the word of Jesus Christ:
  "Come to me, all who labor and are heavy-laden,
  and I will give you rest."
We seek the rest Christ offers,
  for we are often busy and anxious.
Christ invites us, "Take my yoke upon you,
  and learn from me."
There is so much we want to learn about living.
  We want our lives to count for something.
Jesus assures us: "I am gentle and lowly in heart,
  and you will find rest for your souls."
In a harsh world we long for kindness we can trust
  and rest that is truly refreshing.
Again, Christ promises: "My yoke is easy,
  and my burden is light."
In Jesus Christ we find true freedom
  and the joy of living according to the Spirit.
Amen. **Amen.**

CALL TO CONFESSION

We are a people of good intentions who want to accept Christ's invitation.
Indeed, we have done so, many times. However, like the first-century
Christian, whom we know as the apostle Paul, we find that what we want
to do seldom finds fulfillment. Let us use some of Paul's words to make
our confession of sin.

PRAYER OF CONFESSION

I do not understand my own actions, O God of all life. I can will what is
right, but I cannot do it. I do not do the good I want, but the evil I do not
want is what I do. I delight in the law of God, in my inmost self, but with
my flesh I serve the law of sin. Who will deliver me from this body of
death! Hear me and answer, Gracious God! Amen.

ASSURANCE OF FORGIVENESS

God's answer comes again from Paul's writing: There is no condemnation
for those who are in Christ Jesus. We are set free from the law of sin and

death. Live, therefore, according to the Spirit and set your minds on things of the Spirit. To set the mind on the flesh is death, but to set the mind on the Spirit is life and peace. The Spirit of God dwells in you. Believe and celebrate this joyous good news!

COLLECT

Righteous God, we seek your Word, in humility and remorse, recognizing our powerlessness to fulfill our high intentions by ourselves. Like children, who must depend on others for their well-being, we come to you for spiritual nourishment and freedom from bondage to sin and death. May we find life and true peace. Amen.

OFFERTORY PRAYER

Through our offerings, Loving God, we would send to all nations the good news of peace. May we live at peace with one another in this congregation, work for it in our community, and support all efforts to build peace in our homes, in places of work and leisure, and between all hostile forces. To that end, bless and multiply these gifts. Amen.

COMMISSION AND BLESSING

Set your minds on things of the Spirit
    and turn away from self-centered pursuits.
We want to live according to the Spirit,
    putting away all selfishness and sin.
Carry with you the humility of Christ,
    who was gentle and lowly in heart.
We want to follow Christ's example,
    but we fear where it may lead us.
Jesus promised, My yoke is easy
    and my burden is light.
We will need the Spirit's help
    to find comfort in any cross we must bear.
The One who raised Jesus Christ from the dead
    will grant abundant life, fulfilling and eternal.
In Jesus Christ we are finding true freedom
    and the joy of living according to the Spirit.
Amen. Amen.

Eighth Sunday After Pentecost

Old Testament: Exodus 2:11–22
                     Psalm 69:6–15
Epistle: Romans 8:9–17
Gospel: Matthew 13:1–9, 18–23

CALL TO WORSHIP

Welcome, strangers and sojourners, to God's realm,
  where there are no aliens or visitors.
When we are with Christ we know we belong
and our lives have a sense of direction.
Come, all who seek to live by the Spirit,
  who look beyond the needs of the flesh.
When we are slaves to our bodies we die;
  when temporal powers rule us we have no life.
All who are led by the Spirit are God's children,
  heirs through Christ of life with God.
Christ, who was raised from the dead,
  dwells in us and enlivens our spirits.
When we are in Christ we cannot escape the world,
  nor be limited by its narrow understanding of life.
In our zeal to share the wide horizons of God,
  we can bear insult, reproach, and scorn.

INVOCATION

We come to you, O God, an uncertain people. Sometimes we feel like strangers in a foreign land—even in our own homes, our jobs, among acquaintances and friends. We are in the world and often of the world. Yet we sense a part of us reaching for another realm quite unlike our present space. We do not want to escape from the world, nor do we wish to be labeled unbalanced or hysterical. But we long for spiritual depths that will make some sense out of the meaningless mire in which we sometimes lose ourselves. O God, bring all our worlds together and free us to let your Spirit reign in us so we can face life with renewed confidence. Amen.

CALL TO CONFESSION

Our lives are often fragmented by known evil—by jealousy, selfishness, rebellion, cover-up of past deeds. . . . We are not truly free to worship or to live until our relationship with God and others is restored. Let us confess our sin.

PRAYER OF CONFESSION

All-knowing God, there is much inside us, and much we have done, that we would like to hide from you. Sometimes we think no one knows the dark secrets of our hearts. But we know, and you know, the malignant poisons that lurk within, destroying us and undermining our relationships. We cannot live with the fear of being found out. Help us to confess our guilt, face it, make restitution, and go on to live with new freedom and spontaneity, guided by your Spirit. Amen.

ASSURANCE OF FORGIVENESS
Is this not an assurance that can hearten us? "If by the Spirit you put to death the deeds of the body, you will live. . . . You have received the spirit of adoption as heirs." We are freed of our past burdens to respond creatively to our membership in God's family.

COLLECT
May the seed of your Word find good soil in us, Great Sower and Life-Giver. Let not your truth be choked out by competing reverie or swept away by floods of indifference. We want to hear your word and live it in such a way that those who seek and hope in you will not be embarrassed or misled by our life and witness. Amen.

OFFERTORY PRAYER
We are in debt to you, O God, for the food and water that grace our tables and for the spiritual nourishment you offer us day by day. With these gifts we express our gratitude for your abundant provision. Thank you for this opportunity to show our thanks. Amen.

COMMISSION AND BLESSING
Go forth into the world without fear,
   for the Spirit of God dwells in you.
We belong to Christ and our spirits are alive.
   We have been raised with Christ to new vitality.
The Spirit bears witness with our spirits
   that we are children of God.
If we are God's children, we are also heirs,
   heirs of God and joint heirs with Christ.
Christ lived as God intends us to live
   and suffered because he was true to God.
We may have to suffer with Christ
   if we are to know the meaning of Christianity.
Suffering for God can be a joy
   to those who are faithful.
All creation waits with eager longing
   to see the work God's children do.
Amen. **Amen.**

Ninth Sunday After Pentecost

Old Testament: Exodus 3:1–12
Psalm 103:1–13
Epistle: Romans 8:18–25
Gospel: Matthew 13:24–30, 36–43

CALL TO WORSHIP

Bless the Lord, O my soul;
and all that is within me, bless God's holy name!
Bless the Lord, O my soul,
and forget not all God's benefits.
God forgives iniquity and heals disease
and crowns us with steadfast love and mercy.
God satisfies us with good as long as we live,
so our youth is renewed like the eagle's.
God is merciful and gracious,
slow to anger and abounding in steadfast love.
As the heavens are high above the earth,
so great is God's steadfast love toward us.
As parents pity their children,
so the Lord pities those who fear God.
Bless the Lord, O my soul;
and all that is within me, bless God's holy name!

CALL TO CONFESSION

With the whole creation, we bow in awe before the Originator of life, to confess our misuse of the time allotted us, to experience the redemption that is ours in Christ, and to find that freedom in which we can live fully in the present moment. Let us confess our sin.

PRAYER OF CONFESSION

O God of burning bushes, we have chosen to live with dulled eyes and spirits, forgetting your gifts and ignoring your challenges. The cries of your people seldom reach our ears because we insulate ourselves from others' pain. In our insensitivity we miss the flames on your holy ground, for the deeply spiritual experience comes not in splendid isolation, but to those who also care about people. We do not ask for escape from life's difficulties, but for awareness and courage to tackle the tasks you assign us. Help us, today, to produce fruits of the Spirit. Amen.

ASSURANCE OF FORGIVENESS

God does not deal with us according to our sins, nor repay us according to our iniquities. As far as the east is from the west, God removes our transgressions from us. Forgiveness and healing are God's gifts to the truly contrite who enter into God's longing for full realization of creation's intended harmony. We hope for what we have not seen and work for the best we know, with God's blessing. Amen.

COLLECT

Bring us forth, with all your people, to realize the new day you intend. Draw us out of our familiar routines to recognize your presence and your call. Keep us from being weeds in your fields of life or from being so intent on pulling weeds that we hurt a lot of good people along the way. Draw us now into those biblical images that will touch our souls. Amen.

OFFERTORY PRAYER

May these offerings assist in delivering your people from bondage, rescue us from slavery to tradition, and ease and liberate the hungry, abused, and neglected from their oppression. Open our eyes to see the nearby opportunities and practical action we can take to help you start answering our prayer. Amen.

COMMISSION AND BLESSING

God sends us out into the world
   to bring people to the mountaintop.
But we're not ready to explain burning bushes
   or discuss the groaning of creation.
God promises to be with us every step of the way
   to crown us with steadfast love and mercy.
But we want to stay with the sheep, God,
   while you send someone else off to Egypt.
The place where we are standing is holy ground,
   God's tasks for us may be very close at hand.
Sometimes it's hardest to witness among friends,
   to speak a word for God to those who know us best.
Use the gifts God has entrusted to you:
   your eyes, ears, hands, and feet.
We want to be sensitive to God's hurting ones
   and patient in our hope and our service.
Amen. Amen.

Tenth Sunday After Pentecost

Old Testament: Exodus 3:13–20
                    Psalm 105:1–11
Epistle: Romans 8:26–30
Gospel: Matthew 13:44–52

CALL TO WORSHIP

Come before God, asking what you will,
and God will cover your needs.
How can we ask the Ruler of the universe
to give attention to our small problems?
God knows and values you;
nothing is too great or small for God's attention.
Our ancestors in the faith
experienced God's wonderful, rescuing works.
We, too, can know God's care in our lives,
and the trust God appoints us to keep.
We need the food God provides in our wilderness
and the cloud and fire to guide us.
Draw near so the Holy Spirit may encounter you;
hold nothing back from God's All-knowing presence.
We bring all that we have and are
to the throne of grace.
Amen. **Amen.**

CALL TO CONFESSION

Sin is a break in our relationship with the Eternal, rather than simply an accumulation of hurtful acts. The many ways we cut ourselves off from Ultimate Reality keep us from realizing our potential as individuals or as the family of God. Let us reach out to let God bridge the gap we have created. Remember before God what you know is wrong in your life, and ask for help to see the evil you do not recognize. Let us pray.

PRAYER OF CONFESSION

O Sovereign God, we have been so busy with our own pursuits that we have not noticed the treasure hidden in our midst. We have not learned to value things by your standards. We do not see lasting worth in the old we discard, nor have we discovered the dawning merit of much that is new. We are content to live in the ruts of life, rather than climb the mountains of new possibilities. Forgive us, expand our vision, and grant us fresh opportunities to serve your purpose. In Jesus' name. Amen.

ASSURANCE OF FORGIVENESS

In everything, God works for good with those who respond with love and obedience. You bear the image of God, who calls you, justifies you, and glorifies you. Because you have asked for the opportunity to see things God's way, God grants you new strength and a cleansed judgment. Accept God's gift and use it.

COLLECT

We seek to understand your will, O God: to know what is so valuable in life that it is worth all we have and all we are. Grant us discernment to see you at work for good even when events around us seem evil. Nourish us in covenant and set our hearts free to rejoice in Christ's way. Amen.

OFFERTORY PRAYER

We bring no fine pearls or costly treasure to share with the world. But what we bring we dedicate to the search for eternal values. We would be a church that introduces people to the realm of heaven and treats them as your worthy children. Bless each gift, all who give, and every work these offerings support. In Jesus' name. Amen.

COMMISSION AND BLESSING

You are set in the midst of the world's sojourners,
    as people with contributions to make.
We know there are no others just like us,
    nor will the likes of us ever walk the earth again.
You have a distinctive place in God's design;
    your influence extends to places no others can reach.
God will work for the good of many, through us,
    and evil will lose its appeal.
Be alert to the special opportunities
    God sets before you day by day.
We would discern the hidden treasure
    and the pearl of great value.
Be led forth in joy to a new confidence
    in all God will accomplish through you.
We would be righteous and fruitful,
    eschewing dull conformity for wise choices.
Amen. Amen.

Eleventh Sunday After Pentecost

Old Testament: Exodus 12:1–14
(alternate) Nehemiah 9:16–20
Psalm 143:1–10
Epistle: Romans 8:31–39
Gospel: Matthew 14:13–21

CALL TO WORSHIP

Come away to a lonely place for a while
    to sit and learn at the feet of Jesus.
Where Jesus lives we are not lonely,
    for there is compassion and healing power.

In Christ's presence none go hungry,
  but all find bread for body and soul.
Christ is, for us, the bread of life
  and bids us feed our neighbor.
Miracles of sharing are inspired by small gifts,
  spontaneously offered, without pretense or guile.
We want to experience the miracles of Christ,
  beginning in our own attitudes and actions.
Then let Jesus lead you to the Source of life
  and intercede for you before God.
With our sisters and brothers we seek God's blessing,
  in the name of our Savior, Jesus Christ.
Amen. **Amen.**

CALL TO CONFESSION

Through ceremonies and memorials, we find self-discipline and renewal. We neglect them to our peril. When we remember we recognize the deep thirst within our souls. Then we can work at removing the barriers we have erected within us against God. Let us confess our sin.

PRAYER OF CONFESSION

O God, who saved a people from oppression by signs and wonders and an outstretched hand, save us from ourselves and from the perils we face every day. So many stimuli propel us toward the darkness of dishonesty, unfaithfulness, and unfairness. Sometimes we face enemies within—laziness, fear, and low self-esteem. Often structures and powers outside us have little regard for covenant communities, individual rights, or corporate responsibility. We confess our complicity with evil and our slowness to seek your help. Listen to our prayer and deliver us. Amen.

CALL TO CONFESSION (ALTERNATE CONFESSIONAL LITURGY, REFLECTING NEHEMIAH 9:16–20)

The people of Israel, freed from bondage in Egypt, rebelled and sought a leader who would return them to the oppressive known of the past, away from the risky unknown of the future. Unmindful of God's wonders among them, they stiffened their necks, turned away from the commandments, and acted rebelliously. Is it any different for us? Let us confess our sin.

PRAYER OF CONFESSION

We confess, O God, that we resist change, rebel against authority, and refuse to obey. We shape our own idols and find ways to worship them. We turn from the wonders you perform among us and stop our ears against your instructions. When you give us assignments, we look for excuses and declare the tasks impossible. Free us from our self-centered perceptions, limited vision, and spiritual paralysis. We do not like what we see in ourselves and really want to change. Help us! Amen.

ASSURANCE OF FORGIVENESS

God is gracious and merciful, slow to anger, and abounding in steadfast love. God spares nothing to redeem us, even the lifeblood of Jesus Christ, poured out on our behalf. Our Creator meets us where we are—in wilderness, in crowded places, at work, or at worship—with saving grace. God teaches us the way we should go and leads us on a level path. We are set free from sin to live fully as God intends. Praise be to God. Amen.

COLLECT

Gracious God, who provides for us beyond our expectations, remind us of your mighty works amid the great drama of human history. We celebrate your forgiving, reconciling, healing presence, from which nothing can separate us. Multiply the resources we bring to this time and place, that we may participate with you in the compassionate outreach of Jesus Christ. Amen.

OFFERTORY PRAYER

As Christ blessed the loaves and fishes of a generous child in Galilee, we seek your blessing on what we share at this altar. May we, too, with our gifts, be instruments of your purposes. Amen.

COMMISSION AND BLESSING

In love, God justifies and forgives us.
   If God is for us, who can be against us?
Persecution, famine, peril, and sword
   cannot separate us from the love of Christ.
In all things we are more than conquerors
   through the One who loved us.
There is no power on earth, in life or death,
   that can cut us off from God's salvation.
Live, then, as God's children,
   aware of God's generosity and expectations.
As God has blessed us,
   we will share with our neighbors.
Amen. **Amen.**

Twelfth Sunday After Pentecost

Old Testament: Exodus 14:19–31
(alternate) 1 Kings 19:9–18
Psalm 106:4–12
Epistle: Romans 9:1–5
Gospel: Matthew 14:22–33

CALL TO WORSHIP

Welcome to this time of shared prayer,
  when we encourage one another in our ministry.
We need this time for reassurance
  and strengthening for all we face in life.
Here we remember the faith we hold in common
  and find renewal and encouragement.
It is often difficult to sense God's presence
  in the headlines or in our daily contacts.
It is hard to see ourselves as Christ's representatives
  when so few seem to put faith first.
We feel alone and unappreciated,
  as if we were the only faithful ones left.
When everyone marches to a different drummer,
  it is hard to know who's out of step.
Bring us together to hear your still small voice
  so we can recognize you when we're apart.

CALL TO CONFESSION

Life is a mixture of faith and doubts, successes and failures, affirmations and betrayals. Before we can fully appreciate the positive forces at work within and around us, we need to expose the negatives. Let us seek to free ourselves of the sin that clings so closely by seeking God's forgiveness.

PRAYER OF CONFESSION

O God, whom earthquake, wind, and fire cannot contain, we are often shaken by powerful forces on every hand that deny your sovereignty. Our doubts multiply and our faith wearies. We have great sorrow and anguish when we see things as they are with people and nations and try to imagine how they might be if your rule were recognized. It's so lonely out there, with our faith shaken and no one to share it. So we deny you too. Yes, we do, God. And we are sorry. Please forgive us, and help us to try again. Amen.

ASSURANCE OF FAITH

O you of little faith, why do you doubt? There are thousands who share your commitment and continue to renew their trust. Think what this world might be if there were no witness to truth, no workers for peace, no leaders with deep compassion for people, nurtured by their faith. You are making a difference. Your witness is needed and appreciated. God saves you from your foes and delivers you from the power of your enemies. Find gladness and joy in God's steadfast love. Amen.

COLLECT

Mighty God, whom we long to see by some powerful revelation or miraculous intervention, speak to us in a still small voice. We seek you on behalf of the multitudes who need your transforming power, but also for ourselves. Encourage us to take the next step in response to your summons. Reform our doubts, that faith may empower us. Amen.

OFFERTORY PRAYER

O God, it is so simple to give money, even when we have little to share. But it's difficult to put ourselves in the offering plate. That seems to be giving up too much. Is this what you're really asking for? Is it the only way we can ever claim our true selves and find the fulfillment you intend for us? Please answer us, God! Amen.

COMMISSION AND BLESSING

We can stay together no longer;
   there is work for us out in the world.
There is much we do not understand,
   but what we do understand we will do.
We are among God's chosen ones,
   with humble responsibilities unique to us.
God grants us opportunities to serve
   that are available to no others.
God helps us to walk on water when we need to
   and lets us sink when we get too self-centered.
In quiet confidence we face the week ahead,
   listening for the still small voice.
Amen. **Amen.**

Thirteenth Sunday After Pentecost

Old Testament: Exodus 16:2–15
                  Psalm 78:1–3, 10–20
Epistle: Romans 11:13–16, 29–32
Gospel: Matthew 15:21–28

CALL TO WORSHIP

Come to this place of God's visitation and blessing.
Everyone is welcome here.
We are sons and daughters of the new covenant,
disciples of our Sovereign, Jesus Christ.
In Christ there is neither Jew nor Greek,
slave nor free, male nor female.
We are one in Christ, who has chosen us
and equips us for our ministry.
The gifts of God are for no one religion,
and God's family includes all creation.
God's people are of many races and creeds,
old and young, rich and poor, of every land.
We gather to celebrate God's revelation in Jesus,
while others worship the same God in other ways.
We seek to be true to the best we know in Christ,
rejoicing in all faithful service to God.

CALL TO CONFESSION

Sometimes, we are so busy defending beliefs that we fail to see break-downs of trust. Our creeds may blind us to God's inclusiveness and our own unfairness and ingratitude. Our time of confession is an opportunity for us to try to see ourselves as God sees us. Let us pray.

PRAYER OF CONFESSION

Forgive us, O God, for thinking we have you all figured out. We pretend we know who is in and who is out of your family, as if your care were not for all of us. We want people to be like us before we help them, and we welcome into our company only those who will benefit us. We have wandered far from your covenant, overlooked your miracles in our midst, and refused to walk according to your law. Grant that we may keep your commandments because we see their inherent value in helping us to grow in our love toward you, our neighbors, and ourselves. Keep us from treating others as worthless or from murmuring against leaders who move us out of safe ruts into the excitement of following you in word and deed. Amen.

ASSURANCE OF FORGIVENESS

In your disobedience, God's mercy becomes real. In your jealousy and rejection, reconciliation is more meaningful. The gifts and call of God are irrevocable. You have received gifts; you have been chosen for ministry. Fulfill your call. Amen.

COLLECT

We, who claim to be your people, turn to you, O God, to find that inclusive community wherein all are welcome. Reconcile us to your whole family that we might together discover the manna you provide and share it. Show us the streams from which we can drink deeply of faith and abundant life. Amen.

OFFERTORY PRAYER

Through our offerings, we reach out to help people, not because they are "worthy," but because they are your children, in need of what we can share. Thank you for accepting our gifts, inadequate as they may be, and granting us the joy of giving. Amen.

COMMISSION AND BLESSING

You have received the mercy of God;
    now grant mercy to people who wrong you.
We will try to understand the plight of others
    rather than rushing in with judgment.
Be righteous, living by the best you know,
    and just, dealing fairly with others.
We will honor the covenant and magnify our ministry
    in order to improve our human responses.
Let the world see your great faith
    in your humanity and helpfulness.
We seek to be agents of reconciliation
    and carriers of God's peace.
God's grace, mercy, and peace
    equip you for your service in the world. Amen.
Amen.

Fourteenth Sunday After Pentecost

Old Testament: Exodus 17:1–7
                   Psalm 95
Epistle: Romans 11:33–36
Gospel: Matthew 16:13–20

CALL TO WORSHIP

O come, let us worship and bow down,
    let us kneel before God our maker.
O the depth of the riches and wisdom
    and knowledge of God!
Who has known the mind of the Sovereign
    and who has been God's counselor?
In God's hands are the depths of the earth;
    the height of the mountains is God's also.

The sea is God's for God made it;
  and the hands of God formed the dry land.
Make a joyful noise to the rock of our salvation!
  Come into God's presence with thanksgiving.
How unsearchable are God's judgments
  and how inscrutable God's ways!
When we consider the vast reaches of infinity,
  we are moved to awe and wonder.

CALL TO CONFESSION

We come to worship with differing needs. Some of us are alienated from God and people by protective arrogance, and others, by paralyzing fears. Some embrace their talents or education or social standing as evidence of superiority, while others belittle themselves and reject the way God values them. Whatever our particular sin, all of us need forgiveness. Let us seek it together.

PRAYER OF CONFESSION

Mysterious God, we shut out the infinite dimensions and variety of who you are to cut you down to a size we think we can manage. Then we cut ourselves down to stereotypes we can pigeonhole. In this limited view, creativity and spontaneity are snuffed out. Even Jesus becomes a predictable relic of the past. O God, forgive us for so distorting reality that we miss your surprises. Welcome us back to your big world of possibilities. We pray in Jesus' name. Amen.

ASSURANCE OF FORGIVENESS

Blessed are you when you make honest confession and seek to be part of God's wider circle. Move out of the wilderness of sin. You are forgiven, set free, and empowered to live more fully. Praise God! Amen.

COLLECT

God of the prophets and apostles, we recognize that we have been called to join that company of witnesses who serve you on earth. We thirst for living water and a way out of the wilderness of our distorted and limited views. We seek faith to discern your presence and courage to follow the One you sent to lead us, Jesus the Christ. Amen.

OFFERTORY PRAYER

From God and through God and to God are all things. We can give nothing unless we have first received it. We can accomplish nothing except by God's grace. We contribute to no good cause apart from God's purposes. We give thanks for the privilege of giving and refrain from seeking rewards for our generosity. Amen.

COMMISSION AND BLESSING

Go out to be the church,

a faithful, faith-filled people.
We have recognized Christ among us
and belong to the body that bears Christ's name.
Remember the rock of faith on which the church is built,
and find ways to nurture and develop your trust.
The responsibility is ours, together and individually,
to be Christ to our neighbors.
God grants us keys to the realm of heaven,
that we may bind and release in Christ's name.
We can introduce others to the Eternal
and call them, and ourselves, to account.
The power of death shall not prevail
against those who are in Christ Jesus.
We seek to follow the One who was fully human,
in humble obedience and simple trust.
Amen. **Amen.**

Fifteenth Sunday After Pentecost

Old Testament: Exodus 19:1–9
(alternate) Jeremiah 15:15–21
Psalm 114
Epistle: Romans 12:1–13
Gospel: Matthew 16:21–28

CALL TO WORSHIP

God remembers and visits us
and restores us to the community of faith.
In our pain, suffering, and loss
we know the assurance of God's presence.
When we have opposition and hopeless situations,
God bears us up on eagles' wings.
In the loneliness of our firm idealism
God grants healing and transformation.
Whatever we need as we gather to worship,
a merciful and loving God meets us here.
We assemble with high expectations
that God has much good in store for us.
The good gifts God bestows on us here
are for our use in reaching out to others.
We want to use our talents

in the service of Jesus Christ.
Amen. **Amen.**

CALL TO CONFESSION

The apostle Paul appealed to Christians in Rome to "present your bodies as a living sacrifice, holy and acceptable to God, which is your spiritual worship. Do not be conformed to this world but be transformed by the renewal of your mind." Those who take this appeal seriously realize that they fall short of its realization. Join me, in these words or your own thoughts, as we confess our sin.

PRAYER OF CONFESSION

Ever-present God, we have been protective of the gifts you have entrusted to us. We look for our own advantages rather than the well-being of others. We withdraw from those we consider less worthy than we, and court the attention of people who might enhance our position. At the same time, our faith falters in doubt, and we are frozen by our fears. We are often among the opposition rather than on your side, O God. What will it profit us if we gain the whole world but forfeit the fullness of life you intend for us? We need your forgiveness and the gift of new life in Christ. Amen.

ASSURANCE OF FORGIVENESS

Our God, who led people from slavery in Egypt, leads us from our slavery to the worst in ourselves. To all who obey God's voice and keep covenant, the Sovereign One promises a Healing Presence: "You shall be my own possession among all peoples; for all the earth is mine." We are further assured by Jesus that "those who lose their life for my sake will find it." Rejoice in your new freedom and opportunities!

COLLECT

O God, we hear you speaking from a thick cloud, and we are moved to do what you reveal to us. As the one body of your people, we offer our varying gifts in the service of Christ. Before a timeless covenant and a threatening cross, we discern your call to self-denial and sacrificial living. Transform our self-centeredness into compassionate outreach. Help us to live in harmony with all people, to rejoice with those who rejoice, and to weep with those who weep. We would feed our enemies, quench their thirst, and overcome evil with good. Amen.

OFFERTORY PRAYER

We delight once more in the opportunity to give for the cause of Christ. May we contribute generously and give aid, with zeal. Along with our money, we also offer ourselves, as living sacrifices, for the world's transformation. Amen.

COMMISSION AND BLESSING
We go out, not to gain the whole world,
   but to share in its salvation.
We shrink from going to our Jerusalems,
   but we will face their terror with Christ.
Do not be conformed to this world,
   but prove the will of God among people.
We aim to do what is good, acceptable, and perfect,
   but without pretense or conceit.
Use well the gifts of God's grace:
   prophecy, in proportion to your faith,
serving, teaching, and exhortation
   with creativity and enthusiasm,
contributing liberally and aiding zealously,
   doing acts of mercy, with cheerfulness.
Wherever our serving leads,
   we will know God's presence and blessing.
Amen. Amen.

Sixteenth Sunday After Pentecost

Old Testament: Exodus 19:16–24
                 Psalm 115:1–11
Epistle: Romans 13:1–10
Gospel: Matthew 18:15–20

CALL TO WORSHIP
Where two or three gather in Christ's name
   the Sovereign One is present.
Let our coming together proclaim our commitment
   to Christ and the church.
Blow the trumpets to sound God's warning.
   Hold one another accountable before the Creator.
The earth shakes at the visitation of our God,
   and all our idols stand condemned.
God calls us away from our anger and disputes
   to honest communication and reconciliation.
We renew our allegiance to the commandment
   "You shall love your neighbor as yourself."
Amen. Amen.

CALL TO CONFESSION

Sometimes we do not feel like praying. We resist a time of confession as too negative and not really needed. Yet we cling to our idols and to our anger toward other people. Both poison our thoughts and deeds. We need moments to get at "what's eating us," in order to survive. Please join me in prayer—in these words or your own thoughts:

PRAYER OF CONFESSION

O God, we rebel against authority and resist those who would tell us how to live. When we are wronged, we want to fight back. When we are angry with people, we do not want you to forgive them. When we are alienated from others, we prefer to ignore them rather than face the painful process of reconciliation. But you do not let us rest easy with our disputes or our enemies. Down deep we are not happy with ourselves this way. Help us to change, according to your purposes for us. Amen.

ASSURANCE OF FORGIVENESS

When we trust, God is our Help and our Shield. God's wrath is suspended when we come to ourselves and seek forgiveness. God delights in our penitence, forgives our waywardness, and empowers us to turn things around and find newness of life. How wonderful is God's steadfast love and faithfulness!

COLLECT

Our neighbors are part of us, as we seek your word, O God. Some of these neighbors may be enemies. Teach us how to live with them so we may not only know what is right, but also do it. Amen.

OFFERTORY PRAYER

Loving God, sometimes we are like little children who resent having to share their toys. In this mood we are as grudging with our offerings as we are with paying taxes. Help us to see your intention that we be faithful stewards of all you entrust to us. As we "contribute to the needs of the saints," may we hold one another accountable for the wise use of your resources so all we give and all we retain may be used according to your purposes. Amen.

COMMISSION AND BLESSING

Go to your hungry enemies, waiting to be fed,
  and your hurting neighbors who need forgiveness.
Our worship is not complete
  until we have done our all for reconciliation.
Let your church participate with you
  in the building of better relationships.
We seek to live in peace with all people,

and we need the church to help us.
Be affectionately devoted to one another;
outdo one another in showing honor.
**We need help to develop genuine love
in which we really see and hear others.**
Rejoice with those who rejoice,
weep with those who weep.
**We renew our allegiance to the commandment
"You shall love your neighbor as yourself."**
Amen. **Amen.**

Seventeenth Sunday After Pentecost

Old Testament: Exodus 20:1–20
Psalm 19:7–14
Epistle: Romans 14:5–12
Gospel: Matthew 18:21–35

CALL TO WORSHIP

This is the day of our Sovereign God:
let us rejoice and be glad in it.
**All our days belong to our Creator,
and we honor Christ in our thanks for them.**
Let us observe the day in communion with God
and with all our sisters and brothers.
**We open our hearts and lives to our Sovereign
and to those who worship with us.**
None of us live to ourselves,
and none of us die to ourselves.
**If we live, we live to Christ,
and if we die, we die to Christ.**
Jesus reigns over the dead and over the living,
and we must account for ourselves through Christ.
**Let every tongue give praise to God
and every knee bow before God's judgment.**

ALTERNATE CALL TO WORSHIP

Use the psalm for the day.

CALL TO CONFESSION

Some of us are haunted by the evil we have done to others. Some harbor
hatred against a sister or brother. Some of us fear any whose ways are

strange to us. Some are tired of forgiving again and again. All of us are in debt to a loving God who never gives up on us. Let us seek to make things right once more in our relationship with God and all humankind.

PRAYER OF CONFESSION

Good and Patient God, we are back again with the same problem. We are cut off from full communion with you and one another because of our evil thoughts and deeds. We have spoken harshly and judged unfairly those sisters and brothers who need our love. We have inflicted hurt and made unfair demands. Forgive, we pray, the transgressions of your servants, and move us to appreciate your generosity. In thanksgiving for your mercy we offer full pardon and acceptance to those who have wronged us. Amen.

ASSURANCE OF FORGIVENESS

We have this reassurance from God that even our wickedness can be turned to good ends. Those we despise can become friends. When you forgive your brother or sister from the heart, the channels of your own pardon are opened wide. Accept God's gift and live! Amen.

COLLECT

Forgiving God, we, who find it hard to forgive, seek understanding of your good purposes at work, even in the face of evil. Keep us from judging others or nursing grudges. We would extend to all the patience that you have shown toward us. Remove the self-righteous limits we impose when pardoning others, for your grace toward us has far exceeded our deserving. Amen.

OFFERTORY PRAYER

God of all good gifts, we have been all too eager, in our lives, to pay back evil for evil, and slow to pay back your goodness to us. We are so far in debt to you that we can never give enough or do enough to deserve any further consideration from you. Yet you continue to care for us and comfort us, showing mercy and kindness day after day. Receive these offerings as an outpouring of our gratitude. Amen.

COMMISSION AND BLESSING

The week ahead holds hours and days
    that are gifts from God's hand.
They are given to each of us alike
    to enjoy and invest or to hate and destroy.
When we encounter human need
    let us remember how God has met our needs.
In our sisters and brothers in distress
    we meet Christ, who identifies with each one.
We are called to forgive and build up,

to offer mercy in place of harsh judgment.
**In all things God works together for good
with those who receive and extend love.**
Let us go forth rejoicing
and giving ourselves for others.
**We will love in grateful response
to God's forgiving love.**
Amen. **Amen.**

ALTERNATE CLOSE OF WORSHIP

We will have no other gods than the Sovereign One.
We will not make any graven images.
We will not take God's name in vain.
We will keep the sabbath day holy.
We will honor our fathers and mothers.
We will not kill.
We will not commit adultery.
We will not steal.
We will not bear false witness.
We will not covet.
God help us to keep the spirit and intent
of these laws every day!
Amen. Amen.

Eighteenth Sunday After Pentecost

Old Testament: Exodus 32:1–14
  Psalm 106:7–8, 19–22
Epistle: Philippians 1:1–11, 19–27
Gospel: Matthew 20:1–16

CALL TO WORSHIP

Grace to you and peace from God our Parent
and from our Savior Jesus Christ.
**We thank God as we remember one another
and celebrate our partnership in the gospel.**
God has begun a good work among us
and calls for our worthy, wholehearted involvement.
**We will stand side by side, firm in one spirit,
striving for the faith of the gospel.**
Let your life represent the good news,
and enter into fruitful labor on its behalf.

No work of our hands can create anything
worthy of our full devotion.
Recall God's wonderful works and steadfast love
as you seek to do your part.
We will turn away from our golden calves.
It is God who inspires, empowers, and blesses.

CALL TO CONFESSION

We are called to a manner of life worthy of the gospel, a life in which love abounds more and more, with knowledge and all discernment, a life filled with the fruits of righteousness. Because we have a deep sense of our failure to be pure and blameless, we come in humble awe before the One who lived such a life among the likes of us and today can put us in touch with the Eternal.

PRAYER OF CONFESSION

In the name of Jesus Christ, whom we have so often failed to honor in our bodies, we come to confess our corporate and individual guilt. We have been jealous and competitive workers in your vineyard, far more concerned with personal reward than with accomplishing the tasks you set before us. We forget your generosity to us and resent what others receive. Rather than standing side by side for the faith of the gospel, we pursue our separate goals and turn away from true partnership. We even try to create our own little gods. Forgive us, O God, turn us from our grumbling and restore us to fruitful labor and joy in the faith. Amen.

ASSURANCE OF FORGIVENESS

God is understandably angry with our pursuit of lesser gods and our resentment of coworkers. We are a "stiff-necked people" who deserve to be destroyed. But God, in abundant mercy and forgiveness, offers a new start and fresh hope. Let us rejoice in our salvation! Amen.

COLLECT

Gracious God, whose ways are not our ways, we seek your truth. Let your word become so much a part of us that our lives may become worthy of the gospel of Christ. Grant us opportunities to share good news and gratitude to respond generously to all who seek our help. Amen.

OFFERTORY PRAYER

Generous and Loving God, we would not compare the size of our offerings with those of others. Rather, we contrast them with your open-handed provision for us. May we withhold nothing we have to give from involvement in your purposes for this planet. Amen.

COMMISSION AND BLESSING

Stand firm in one spirit, with one mind
striving side by side for the faith of the gospel.

For us to live is Christ and to die is gain,
  so we will serve without fear or complaint.
Let your manner of life
  be worthy of the gospel.
We will share the good news with others
  by what we do and in all we say.
Let your prayers and conversations
  be filled with joy and thanksgiving.
We will hold our sisters and brothers
  in our hearts, upholding their ministry.
Grace to you and peace from God our Parent
  and from the Sovereign Jesus Christ. Amen.
Amen.

Nineteenth Sunday After Pentecost

Old Testament: Exodus 33:12–23
                  Psalm 99
Epistle: Philippians 2:1–13
Gospel: Matthew 21:28–32

CALL TO WORSHIP
  The Eternal One summons us from work to worship,
    from dull monotony to high adventure.
  We are called to look beyond life's routines
    to their meaning and possibilities.
  God satisfies us in the morning with steadfast love,
    that we may rejoice and be glad all our days.
  As we participate in the Spirit,
    our selfish conceits give way to unity.
  The mind of Christ prompts humility within
    and kindly service to those who need us.
  God is at work with us
    to accomplish Eternal purposes.
  Then let us worship God with joy and praise,
    knowing our salvation is in Christ.
  The turmoil of life's everyday fragmentation
    is calmed as we rediscover our wholeness.
  Amen. **Amen.**

CALL TO CONFESSION
  Many centuries ago the psalmist cried out to God: "You have set our

iniquities before you, our secret sins in the light of your countenance. We are consumed by your anger and overwhelmed by your wrath." When we are feeling guilty, God may loom over us as a frightening judge. Yet God invites us to turn back from our sin and be freed from it. God listens and responds. God forgives. Let us seek God in prayer.

PRAYER OF CONFESSION

Sovereign God, just when we think we have buried our wickedness from everyone's view, you expose it and call us to deal with it openly and courageously. We have not treated others with the sympathy and kindness you expect. Insead, we have used them for our own ends. We have been selfish, conceited, and arrogant, putting our own interests first. We play god as we grasp and manipulate things and people. O God, turn us inside out, and replace the demons inside us with your own loving spirit. We pray in Jesus' name. Amen.

ASSURANCE OF FORGIVENESS

All who turn away from wickedness and do what is right shall be saved. I have no pleasure in the death of anyone, says the Sovereign God, so turn and live. God is at work in you, both to will and to work for God's good pleasure.

COLLECT

When you address us, O God, keep us from turning away. When we make commitments, help us to follow through. When our actions condemn us, recall us to yourself and grant us a new heart and a new spirit. We open ourselves to your work among us and through each one of us. Show us your glory and grant us to partake of your goodness. Amen.

OFFERTORY PRAYER

Put these gifts, and our time and talents, to work in your vineyard, Sovereign God. Grant to us the capacity to move beyond good intentions to give ourselves completely to the purposes of your realm. Amen.

COMMISSION AND BLESSING

The Eternal One sends us back to our daily work
with renewed inspiration and motivation.
We see fresh ways to improve the quality of life
for ourselves and all companions on this earth.
We are moved by sympathy and affection
to listen and respond more fully.
We do not need to protect false images
but can be ourselves with other people.
The strength we find in being together
goes with us as we part to serve.
We are committed anew to God's purposes
and confident we have something to give.

The Pentecost Season   115

The vineyards of life summon us
   with much that needs to be done.
We will go where God sends us
   and do the work God equips us to do.
Amen. Amen.

Twentieth Sunday After Pentecost

Old Testament: Numbers 27:12–23
(alternate)   Isaiah 5:1–7
                   Psalm 81:1–10
Epistle: Philippians 3:12–21
Gospel: Matthew 21:33–43

CALL TO WORSHIP
Sing to the God who loves us,
   who blesses us with unlimited possibilities.
Praise God, the source of all good gifts,
   who provides for us beyond all expectations.
God clears away the debris from our lives,
   making us good soil for God's word.
God removes the obstructing stones
   and prepares us to live God's truth.
The church is God's vineyard,
   and each of us, God's pleasant planting.
The rich harvest God expects
   is a community of justice and peace.
We are to bear good fruit befitting God's realm,
   to offer nourishment, lest any faint of hunger.
How can we meet the high expectations
   of a God beyond the reach of our imagination?

CALL TO CONFESSION
Come to the God who meets us in our failures, as well as our successes,
who is ready to hear us when we confess our guilt, who judges our
hypocrisy but forgives the sincerely penitent. Let us pray, individually
and then together, using word-symbols to utter the inexpressible.

PRAYER OF CONFESSION
God of all life's vineyards, we have claimed what is yours as our own, to be
used for our selfish benefit. Your good seed has, in us, yielded wild
grapes. Where there should be enough for all your children, we have

116   The Pentecost Season

hoarded your gifts until they have turned sour for us and too rotten to be shared. Our bellies have become our gods, and our minds are set on earthly things. We find no glory in the cross of Christ, for we have lived as its enemies. Who can save us from this body of death, for we have rejected and murdered the heir you sent among us? Amen.

ASSURANCE OF FORGIVENESS

To the unfaithful keepers of the vineyard, Jesus said, "The realm of God will be taken away from you and given to a nation producing the fruits of it." We can move so far away from God's purposes that we bring that judgment on ourselves. But to all who, in serious penitence, turn to the commonwealth of heaven as their home, God issues a Parent's welcome. We are forgiven! Let us forget what lies behind and strain forward to what lies ahead. Amen.

COLLECT

From the midst of all the lesser gods of life in which we find delight, we sing aloud to God, our strength. We do not want to be enemies of the cross or unfaithful servants who reject Truth. Offer to us anew, we pray, the realm in which your will is supreme. Lay your hands upon us that we may be people in whom your Spirit dwells. Open our ears to hear the goals Christ sets before us. Amen.

OFFERTORY PRAYER

O God, you are owner of all we possess. We open our mouths and you fill them. Life itself is your gift to us. We would return to you now the fruits of our labor, in joyous thanksgiving for the privilege of managing a small portion of your vineyard. May we and our offerings be subject to Christ in all things. Amen.

COMMISSION AND BLESSING

Press on toward the goal for the prize
   of the upward call of God in Christ Jesus.
We will no longer live for lesser goals
   that are unworthy of our efforts.
God grants greater maturity and daring
   as you accept challenges not before considered.
We are awed by God's trust in us
   yet eager to explore the new vistas before us.
Your Savior greets you from heaven's commonwealth,
   welcoming your renewed participation.
How good it is to labor in God's realm,
   to set our minds on eternal values.
May the Spirit empower you
   to live fully, as God's own children.

We will be true to the best we know
and open to increased understanding.
Amen. Amen.

Twenty-first Sunday After Pentecost

Old Testament: Deuteronomy 34:1–12
Psalm 135:1–14
Epistle: Philippians 4:1–20
Gospel: Matthew 22:1–14

CALL TO WORSHIP

We have come again to the mountain
where God's presence is made known.
We are here to praise our Creator,
for God has done wonderful things.
God makes clouds, lightning, and rain
and brings forth the wind from God's storehouse.
God sent signs and wonders to save people
from the oppression of the Egyptians.
God's name endures forever
among those on whom God's hand has rested.
We rejoice in gifts of wisdom and truth
and in the compassion God extends to us.
Bring thanksgiving and supplication to God,
who hears and answers our prayers.
God has been our refuge and strength
and will supply everything we need.

CALL TO CONFESSION

God invites us to the marriage feast of life, but we put off accepting the invitation. We are summoned to celebrate the love of Jesus Christ, but we busy ourselves with other distractions. Surely, God will judge our unresponsive dalliance. Let us examine ourselves and seek forgiveness.

PRAYER OF CONFESSION

God of hosts, we have made light of your invitation to participate fully in your family. We live as if we were not dependent on you for everything we enjoy and for life itself. We have treated our brothers and sisters as enemies rather than friends. Deceit reigns in place of truth, and scandal replaces honor. Through injustice, uncleanness, ugliness, insolence, and mediocrity we deny Christ and the witness of generations of Christians. On our own initiative we are powerless to change. Help us, O God. Free us from the sin that weighs us down, and equip us to do what we have learned from you. Amen.

ASSURANCE OF FORGIVENESS

God judges the sincerity of our prayers. "Many are called, but few are chosen," Jesus said. The chosen ones are surely those who have accepted God's rule in their lives and have broken with their old destructive willfulness. All who confess their sin with eagerness to accept God's sovereignty are freed from their old burdens of guilt. Rejoice greatly in the renewed strength Christ gives. Amen.

COLLECT

In gratitude, we join our ancestors in the faith in thanking you for your provision of all that we need. Where we have been unmindful of your generosity, fill us with new awareness of truth, honor, justice, purity, loveliness, graciousness, and excellence. May we never take lightly your invitation to the feast of life, where we hear your word and do it. Amen.

OFFERTORY PRAYER

May our gifts be acceptable and pleasing to you, O God, for we present ourselves in a partnership of giving and receiving. We have enjoyed the bounty you provide; grant us now the depth of commitment we need to sacrifice all else for the privilege of serving you. In Jesus' name. Amen.

COMMISSION AND BLESSING

Rejoice in the Sovereign always;
  again, I will say, rejoice!
God has met us here and blessed us;
  we give thanks for God's abundant kindness.
You have been equipped to face life
  in all its ambiguities and anguish.
We know how to be abased
  and how to abound.
In plenty and hunger, abundance and want,
  we are not alone.
We can do all things
  through Christ, who strengthens us.
The peace of God, which passes all understanding,
  keep your hearts and minds in Christ Jesus.
To God, our Mother and Father,
  be all glory forever and ever.
Amen. **Amen.**

Twenty-second Sunday After Pentecost

Old Testament: Ruth 1:1–19a
(alternate) Isaiah 45:1–7
 Psalm 146
Epistle: 1 Thessalonians 1:1–10
Gospel: Matthew 22:15–22

CALL TO WORSHIP

God has chosen us and called us by name,
 grasped us by the hands and opened doors for us.
It is flattering to be recognized by name
 and to have opportunities open up before us.
But we are fearful of a God who acts decisively
 to touch us and lead us in God's own way.
Where will God have us go,
 and how can we make our way in unknown places?
"I am God, and beside me there is no other;
 I gird you though you do not know me."
We hear God declaring sovereignty over all things
 and offering to prepare us for life's encounters.
From the rising of the sun, God will be known,
 in both light and gloom, weal and woe.
We worship a God who reigns over all things
 and offers support to us, who are God's creation.

CALL TO CONFESSION

If God were passive or absent, we could ignore God and live to ourselves. But God acts, and we often respond in fear or rebellion. In our private retreats from life we cut ourselves off from God and other people. God does not force us out of our miserable isolation, but the hand of assurance and welcome is extended to us, awaiting our response. I invite you to pray with me, in words and in silence.

PRAYER OF CONFESSION

Where are you leading us, God? What if we do not want to go? We do not trust you, for much in life has not been the way we want it to be. We hold you responsible for our misery. Why don't you intervene to make life better for us? For all people? Let us tell you a few improvements you could make . . .

O God, our vision is so limited. Please do not punish us by giving us all we think we want. You are so great, so much more than we can imagine. We have tried to play god and end up feeling more wretched than before.

Forgive us, O God. Turn us around inside. Help us to cope with the way
_things are, so we can follow Christ in working to make a few things the
way you want them to be. Amen.

ASSURANCE OF FORGIVENESS
"I will go before you and level the mountains," says our God. The Holy
One hears our cries, affirms us even when we are in rebellion or retreat,
leads us away from the idols we create, and forgives us when we turn from
our own ways to open ourselves to God's purposes. Receive the new life
Christ has brought among us. Amen.

COLLECT
We hear you call our name, O God, our Mother and Father, and want to
follow you, even into unknown places. You know our faith, our love, our
steadfastness. You also know our devious designs and our hypocrisy.
Grant that, as we hear the gospel, we may know again the power of your
Holy Spirit transforming our lives and informing all our decisions. Amen.

OFFERTORY PRAYER
We have rendered to Caesar much that we do not care to give, O God.
Now we return to you the gifts that are yours. All our wealth and
possessions belong to you. Bless our use of these resources, both what we
bring for the church's ministry and outreach and what we keep to support
ourselves and provide for those we love most. Amen.

COMMISSION AND BLESSING
Return to your worlds, guided by the Word
  and empowered by the Holy Spirit.
Do not leave us, O Living and True God,
  or keep us from following after you.
The company of your people will be our people,
  and you will always be our God, even in death.
We have heard God call our names,
  so we dare to trust God's leading.
Uphold your brothers and sisters in your prayers
  and support one another in faith, hope, and love.
We will be channels of God's care
  for those we love and all we meet.
Grace to you and peace, from the rising of the sun
  to the going down of the same.
We have received and rejoice in God's blessing.
  All praise and thanks to the Triune God!
Amen. **Amen.**

Twenty-third Sunday After Pentecost

Old Testament: Ruth 2:1–13
Psalm 128
Epistle: 1 Thessalonians 2:1–8
Gospel: Matthew 22:34–46

CALL TO WORSHIP

Turn from your idols to recognize the One True God;
the Creator of the universe is with us here.
We celebrate the nearness of the Living God,
whom all time and space cannot contain.
God meets you in this place, this hour,
and in all your yesterdays and tomorrows.
We cannot travel beyond the reach of God's love
or escape the intensity of God's wrath.
Widows, orphans, sojourners, and poor folk,
come to meet the Compassionate One.
God meets our needs as a Gentle Nurse
and silences critics with a word of love.
Let us celebrate with joy and gratitude
the deliverance God offers in Jesus Christ.
We will lift our voices to declare our faith
and renew our commitment to share ourselves.

CALL TO CONFESSION

We, whose hearts, souls, and minds have dwelt this week on our own
survival, are summoned in these moments to expand the range of our
concerns. We, whose anger is stirred by those who have more of the
world's goods than we—or by those who, in seeming laziness, waste the
substance our hard work has provided them—all of us jealous and self-
protective folk are invited to recognize our own sinfulness. Let us pray.

PRAYER OF CONFESSION

Generous God, we have been greedy and selfish with the things of this
world and even with the love you have poured out among us. We have
viewed life around us through the narrow focus of our own immediate
self-interest, without awareness of people who are used and abused as we
grab for what we want. O God, test our hearts, turn us from our unconscious distortions and our conscious deceits, and bring us to fuller acceptance of your life-changing forgiveness. In Jesus' name. Amen.

ASSURANCE OF FORGIVENESS

Hear and believe the gospel. Jesus Christ delivers us from the wrath to come. You are forgiven, approved by God, and entrusted with the love that restores you to full communion with your Sovereign. Blessed is everyone who fears God and walks in God's way. Share the good news!

COLLECT

Entrust us again with the gospel of Jesus Christ, that we may love you with all our being and our neighbors as ourselves. We would risk opposition to serve you faithfully. We want to identify with the poor and oppressed for whom you have special compassion. Guide us by your word to share ourselves, along with your good news. Amen.

OFFERTORY PRAYER

With our gifts we proclaim the gospel of Jesus Christ, knowing that the good news we take to the world is muted not so much by active opposition, as by our passive disregard. May the act of giving inspire us to invest ourselves anew in the programs and people you want us to reach with your love. Amen.

COMMISSION AND BLESSING

You have heard again the great commandments:
    take them with you and live by them.
We will love the Sovereign God
    with all our heart, soul, and mind.
Do you mean that? Will you live to please God?
    Will the love of God come first in your life?
We will love the Sovereign God
    with all our heart, soul, and mind.
When you do that, everything in the world changes.
    People will nevermore be confused with things.
We will do no wrong to our sisters and brothers;
    we will love our neighbors as ourselves.
Do you mean that? Is it your full intent?
    Will love dominate all your thoughts and actions?
We will love God with all our heart, soul, and mind,
    and we will love our neighbors as ourselves.
Amen. **Amen.**

Twenty-fourth Sunday After Pentecost

Old Testament: Ruth 4:7–17
                    Psalm 127
Epistle: 1 Thessalonians 2:9–13, 17–20
Gospel: Matthew 23:1–12

CALL TO WORSHIP

What is your purpose for gathering in this place?
  Why have you come before the God of hosts?
We are here to honor God and entreat God's favor.
  How great is God's name among all the nations!
Do you really mean what you are saying?
  How have you kept covenant with your Creator?
We have been Christians as long as we can remember;
  we come to church, teach, and bring offerings.
Do your actions proclaim life, joy, and peace?
  Do you practice what you say you believe?
We are weary of being questioned and insulted;
  surely, our behavior is as good as most others'!
God is not pleased with less than our best
  or honored by our tainted sacrifices.
God knows us better than we know ourselves.
  May God help us to be worthy listeners!

CALL TO CONFESSION

To those who cut corners in the practice of their faith, who worshiped without passion and gave without true generosity, the prophet spoke for God: "I have no pleasure in you and I will not accept an offering from your hand. . . . I will curse your blessings. . . . I will put you out of my presence." What have we to say to a God who is angry with our half-hearted commitments?

PRAYER OF CONFESSION

God of hosts, we, your children, have not accorded you the honor due a parent or the respect a servant owes the one who is served. We have polluted your name with our pretenses of goodness, for we do not practice what we preach. Others observe us and are turned away from Christ by what they see. We have cheated you and others by withholding our best for ourselves. We covet positions of honor and chase after public recognition. Our good deeds are designed more to impress the right people than to help needy ones. We have been faithless to one another, eating the bread of anxious toil. O God, we are sorry that we have caused others to stumble. We beg you to pardon us and restore us to your service. Amen.

ASSURANCE OF FORGIVENESS

As you humble yourselves in awe before the Almighty, God hears you and trusts your sincerity. Your life is restored by God's goodness and mercy. Shut the doors against halfhearted and faithless living. Open yourselves to live as God's own children, pledging and giving your best. Share yourselves with one another as forgiven and forgiving people.

COLLECT

We turn again to our faith heritage as a mirror in which to see ourselves as we really are. Where we are giving less than our best, O God, convict us. When we have been faithless to you and to one another, renew in us the covenant that binds us together. As we challenge others to service and sacrifice, but shrink from the same standards for ourselves, humble us and empower us to practice what we preach. Amen.

OFFERTORY PRAYER

These offerings are part of ourselves—our work, our investment of time and resources. We give thanks for your abundant blessings that make it possible for us to share. We would not cheat you by withholding our best, either at your altar or in our daily encounters with your children. Help us to grow in worthiness of your continuing favor. Amen.

COMMISSION AND BLESSING

Are you ready to face another week?
   Have your purposes for gathering been fulfilled?
God has spoken to us once more
   a message we need to hear.
Will you keep covenant with your Creator,
   whose blessings are for all, without partiality?
Are we not all children of one God?
   Has not one God created us?
Live, then, in faithfulness to one another
   and to the God who calls forth your service.
Christ is our teacher, who lifted others' burdens.
   We are learning from Christ to do the same.
All who exalt themselves will be humbled,
   and all who humble themselves will be exalted.
The word of God is at work in us,
   and we witness to it in word and deed.
Amen. **Amen.**

Twenty-fifth Sunday After Pentecost

Old Testament: Amos 5:18–24
                 Psalm 50:7–15
Epistle: 1 Thessalonians 4:13–18
Gospel: Matthew 25:1–13

CALL TO WORSHIP

This is the day and the hour of God's coming
   with justice and righteousness, hope and comfort.

We come for both judgment and reassurance
   because we are unfaithful and we are needy.
There is brightness and shadow around us,
   both light and gloom within.
Sometimes we are wise and sometimes foolish,
   sometimes watchful, at other times careless.
In all places and conditions God is with us:
   in grief and sorrow and in our celebrations.
When it seems we flee lions and are met by bears,
   even God may appear to us a biting serpent.
When we are called to serve and fail to prepare,
   doors may be closed to us.
When we live as if there were no God,
   we may hear no response when we call for help.

CALL TO CONFESSION

Often we gather in solemn assemblies, hoping that God will overlook our true intentions. We expect to go through our usual routines without being challenged or changed. God sees through our pretensions and invites us to face ourselves and the nature of our sin. Let us pray.

PRAYER OF CONFESSION

God of justice and righteousness, we have twisted your rules for humanity to accommodate our advantages. We play our own songs, ignoring the discord we create in your symphony of life. We put off any changes in our attitudes or conduct, taking advantage of your patience and willingness to forgive. Grab hold of us now, O God, while we still have the capacity to change. We do not want to be shut out of your festival of life. Amen.

ASSURANCE OF FORGIVENESS

Do not grieve as those who have no hope. All who are in Christ will rise again to new life. Call on God in your day of trouble, and God will deliver you. Trim your lamps and prepare to share fully in the service to which God appoints you. God has high expectations for you, hurts when you hurt, and sympathizes with all who are poor and oppressed. Let justice roll down like waters and righteousness like an ever-flowing stream.

COLLECT

Touch our inmost being, O God, for our solemn assemblies have no meaning without the change of heart that moves us to faithful actions. Equip us with oil for our lamps, hope in the midst of grief, and high purpose when we are weighed down by despair. We want to be instruments of your justice and peace, however costly the implementation. Amen.

OFFERTORY PRAYER

Eternal God, we bring offerings, not because you require them, but because we want to express our thanks; not to fulfill the law, but to demonstrate love; not to fund our pet programs, but to help others experience your justice and righteousness. Use these gifts to bring comfort to those who grieve, meaning to all whose vision is clouded, freedom to the oppressed, and food for all who hunger. Please accept and multiply these offerings to the benefit of everyone who receives and all who give. Amen.

COMMISSION AND BLESSING

As we go our separate ways, God is with us,
and we awaken each morning to a day of God.
We cannot escape God's judgment
or wander beyond the reach of God's care.
Be prepared for Christ's coming among us
and patient in your waiting and serving.
Our lamps are lighted against life's shadows,
to illumine the way of our Sovereign.
Find ways to lift the heavy loads people carry,
and do not add to your neighbor's burden.
Our sisters' grief is our own,
and our brothers' sorrow calls forth our tears.
Do not grieve as those who have no hope,
for God's trumpets will call us to a new day.
We will stand with one another to give comfort
and hold before one another our hope in Christ.
Amen. **Amen.**

Twenty-sixth Sunday After Pentecost

Old Testament: Zephaniah 1:7, 12–18
                   Psalm 76
Epistle: 1 Thessalonians 5:1–11
Gospel: Matthew 25:14–30

CALL TO WORSHIP

Be silent before the Sovereign God!
For the day of God is at hand.
We will put aside all that distracts us
from our worship and service.
On those who are oblivious to their sin,
God's jealous wrath is poured out.
Take away the gloom and anguish,

the clouds and threat of devastation.
God's distress with us is very real,
and our punishment is deserved.
**We do not want to be children of the night
who must hide our actions from others.**
Turn, then, from the shadows of sin
to respond to the glowing lamps of God's love.
**We seek God's face amid the poor and needy
and open our hands to feed the hungry.**

CALL TO CONFESSION

The God who loves us also calls us to account. We whose senses are dulled in so many destructive ways have failed to see God in action in our own history. We have placed our trust in silver and gold rather than in God's saving activity. While there is yet some life within us, let us turn away from what has been, to embrace God's exciting new possibilities.

PRAYER OF CONFESSION

What shall we do, God, when life overwhelms us and we are afraid to risk the little of value we see in ourselves? We confess that we have hidden our talents and protected ourselves. Your expectations of us overwhelm us and we feel helpless before your judgment. We do not want to feel this way or to run from situations we cannot handle. Where is there good news for us? Will you help us climb out of the depths of fear and despair? Help us be faithful in our use of whatever you entrust to us. Amen.

ASSURANCE OF FORGIVENESS

God has not destined us for wrath, but to obtain salvation through our Sovereign Jesus Christ. God wills good and not harm for all of us. When we come in penitence and trust, we open the lines of communication and blessing that our selfish pursuits cut off. Live now as forgiven people, united by faith, love, and mutual encouragement.

COLLECT

Sovereign God, to whom belongs all we have and all we are, we pray for insight and will to use well all that you have entrusted to us. May we be worthy of others' trust, generous to those who are in need, and full of encouragement for our sisters and brothers in the faith. Inspire us to such selfless service that we may be surprised by your commendation, "Well done, good and faithful servant!" Amen.

OFFERTORY PRAYER

We bring before you, O God, this accounting of our faithfulness. You have entrusted much to us. We return some of it for the work of your church. Grant us imagination and generosity to use all you entrust to us in ways that build up rather than destroy. Amen.

COMMISSION AND BLESSING

To those who have used well the gifts of God,
the Sovereign One entrusts greater responsibility.
It is a joy to serve God through serving others,
to build up and encourage our neighbors.
Live as children of the day, worthy of trust
and dependable in your outreach.
Our deeds are open to God's searching light,
and we will not shrink from God's judgment.
In silence and in speech
let your witness be true.
In all our works we would praise God
and in all relationships value God's children.
May God's mercy continue and save this earth
from death and destruction.
May all our attitudes and actions be life-affirming
and supportive of genuine peace among people.
Amen. Amen.

Last Sunday After Pentecost

Old Testament: Ezekiel 34:11–16, 20–24
                   Psalm 23
Epistle: 1 Corinthians 15:20–28
Gospel: Matthew 25:31–46.

CALL TO WORSHIP

God calls together the scattered flock,
searching for all who have wandered away.
We have strayed from God's purposes
and yet resist the idea that we must be rescued.
God brings us home and feeds our spirits.
God binds up our wounds and strengthens the weak.
It is good to be at home in God's house
and to be reminded of how much God cares for us.
God, in Christ, calls us to grow up and bear fruit,
to share with the Chosen One in resurrection victory.
We long to be raised from the death that engulfs us,
to live in newness of life under God's rule.
Worship God with renewed intent to share in ministry
to the least of our sisters and brothers in need.

We come to this time and place for renewed vision,
deepened intent, and empowerment to act.

INVOCATION

Monarch of all worlds and Judge of all who share this planet, we know you
are with us here. We sense the majesty and power with which you rule
over all things. We also claim the warmth of your love, which reaches out
to the least and the lost with good news. May we be participants in your
grace and instruments of your eternal purposes. Grant us the capacity to
share without counting the cost. In Christ's name. Amen.

PRAYER OF CONFESSION

Sovereign God, all we, like sheep, have gone astray. We have turned to
the ways of death rather than of life. We have preferred security to
sacrifice and gluttony to generosity. We have failed to care about or
respond to the needs of our sisters and brothers, for we have been
preoccupied with our own narrow concerns. Forgive us and turn us
around so we may accept our rightful place in your eternal realm. Amen.

ASSURANCE OF FORGIVENESS

"As in Adam all die, so also in Christ shall all be made alive." We are a
new people, equipped with fresh vision and purpose to reach out as
Christ's hands and feet, ministering to a needy world. Leave behind your
self-imposed limitations and give your best to the one who needs what
you have to give.

COLLECT

We, who have been rescued and fed, bound up and strengthened, would
hear again your challenge, O God, to live life to its fullest. We recognize
you as the Source of life and the Provider of new life in Jesus Christ. May
we put you first in our attention as we reach out to feed the hungry, clothe
the naked, welcome the stranger, heal the sick, and minister to prisoners.
In Jesus' name. Amen.

OFFERTORY PRAYER

On behalf of those who are hungry, thirsty, alone, and friendless, we offer
our gifts and ourselves. Help us to claim our kinship with all your
children and to participate with you in that work through which all of us
were redeemed and reconciled and made whole. Amen.

COMMISSION AND BLESSING

Scatter again into the world,
but do not lose your way.
We seek to follow where our shepherd leads
and to find nourishment where God provides.

Seek the light and do not dwell in the shadows.
Ask for the help you need, day by day.
**We know we are not alone,
for God is everything to us and trusts us.**
Fulfill the trust placed in you, by responding
to the cries of your sisters and brothers.
**We will share what we have with the needy
and give ourselves with our gifts.**
Follow Christ in a new life of service
that bears fruit among all you meet.
**We accept Christ's empowering presence
in our midst and in our own hearts.**
Amen. **Amen.**

Thanksgiving Day

Old Testament: Deuteronomy 8:7–18
Psalm 65
Epistle: 2 Corinthians 9:6–15
Gospel: Luke 17:11–19

CALL TO WORSHIP

God crowns our year with bounty.
The hills and valleys sing for joy.
**The meadows are clothed with flocks
and the fields are decked with grain.**
The whole land drips with fatness,
for God has richly prospered us.
**God brought our ancestors to a good land,
and we have benefited from their labors.**
Praise is due to God who has answered our prayers,
who fills all the ends of the earth with hope.
**God has provided every blessing in abundance
so we have more than enough to share.**
We will not forget the source of our plenty
or take for granted what God entrusts to us.
**We shall eat and be full, and thank God
for the generosity we can pass on.**
Amen. **Amen.**

INVOCATION

We pour out our thanksgiving, Gracious God, for this land of richness and
beauty, overflowing with trees, grain, fruit, and resources of every kind.

Prayer of Prep
11/18/90

The Pentecost Season   131

The good earth has yielded abundant harvests and supported commerce and industry unimagined by our forebears. In times of trial and deepest need your hand has sustained us. Your mercy, undeserved and often unappreciated, has been with us in many difficult places. On this special day we pause to name all for which we are grateful. . . . Amen.

CALL TO CONFESSION

In the book of Deuteronomy we are warned: "Beware lest you say in your heart, 'My power and the might of my hand have gotten me this wealth.' You shall remember your God, who has given you power to get wealth." Christianity is a materialistic religion. Jesus talked about money and possessions more than most other subjects. Religion is not a compartment of life, but is concerned with the whole of life, much of which involves the things we accumulate. Those things can become ends in themselves rather than tools in the service of God and humanity. They can be vehicles for self-centered pride rather than carriers of God's good news. Thanksgiving Day is a good time to ponder our management of God's wealth, entrusted to our stewardship. Let us pray.

PRAYER OF CONFESSION

Almighty God, when we move beyond sentimentality to recognize who you really are, we are filled with awe and terror. Our spiritual ancestors spoke of your dread deeds against all who defied your purposes. We realize you have reason to be angry with us, for we have not put your will first in our lives. We have lived without gratitude and misused the good gifts you have made available. We even forget that you are the source of all things and imagine that we have come to the place where we are by our own efforts. Draw us back to yourself, O God, not to chasten, but to lead. Have mercy on us, and receive our thanks. Amen.

ASSURANCE OF FORGIVENESS

The One who supplies seed to the sower and bread for food will supply and multiply your resources and increase the harvest of your righteousness. You will be enriched in every way for great generosity, which will produce thanksgiving to God. Your cries are heard; your longing for restoration and full participation in the realm of God is answered. Rise and go your way; your faith has made you whole.

COLLECT

Generous God, we are thankful for your Word, which meets us through words of long ago that we can read today. We acknowledge the gospel of Christ and seek to live in generous response to it. Equip us to take from the courts of your holy temple the initiative to give to the poor and to return again and again to pour out our thanks. Amen.

OFFERTORY PRAYER

Loving God, we would sow bountifully that we may also reap bountifully.

We give cheerfully and not out of compulsion, in response to the generous outpouring of abundance we have received from your hand. Giving
helps us to appreciate more fully your giving to us. Our giving produces
more and more thanksgiving within us. Thanks be to you, O God, for
your inexpressible gift in Christ! Amen.

COMMISSION AND BLESSING

L May thanksgiving be more than a special day;
   may it be for you a way of life.

G **We have been enriched in every way**
   for great generosity and thanksgiving to God.

L Appreciate anew the good earth
   that is our inheritance from a loving God.

P **We celebrate again God's goodness to our ancestors**
   and God's continuing provision for us.

L The God who has answered our prayers
   asks our help in answering the prayers of others.

P **We will not forget the source of our good life** — *God our Maker, our*
   ~~or think we can keep it by hoarding it.~~ *Keeper, and our*
   Redeemer.

   God, who raised mountains and stills roaring seas,
   will dwell with you to calm and uplift.

   Grant us, O God, to live peaceably with all you love
   and with thankfulness at the heart of all we do.
   Amen. Amen.

Appendix
of Related Hymn Texts

A new hymn text is provided for each occasion in the church year, based on one or more of the suggested scriptures for the day. There are a few additional general and seasonal offerings. All these hymns are identified by meter. By consulting the metrical index in any standard hymnal, one can find a number of tunes to which these words may be sung. Anyone planning worship should sing through the hymn in its entirety or consult with a musician who can test the appropriateness of the selected tune. Because of the placement of verbal accents and the varied musical construction of tunes bearing the same meter, not every tune of the indicated meter will match the words.

These hymn texts (as well as the worship materials) may be copied in church bulletins for use in worship services. Their source in this book is to be acknowledged, along with the name of the author. Unless otherwise noted, the hymns were written by Lavon Bayler. (See page iv for the exact credit line to be used.) A topical index will alert you to additional hymns that may be appropriate for the service you are planning. It is hoped that you will be encouraged to author an occasional hymn and compose new tunes if that is your gift. Eliciting these talents from others is also important.

This book does not address the need for contemporary musical expression in worship. Many youth of my acquaintance, and some adults as well, find the traditional tunes foreign to their experience and taste. Although I would not want us to discard the stately music of the past, I encourage the expansion of our musical repertoire. Creative experimentation in your church, using talents never before tapped, may make worship come alive to many more people.

Hymns for the Advent Season

1. Awaken, My People

Advent 1   *S.M. 6.6.8.6.*

Awaken, my people,
Watch with God now in prayer.
Know that Christ comes in human form
To call forth love and care.

It is God's gift of love
That breaks our swords in two,
And plowshares into pruning hooks,
To see God's larger view.

Visit your people soon
That love may win the day.
On mountaintops, through valleys low,
Make ours a peaceful way.

Advent new vision brings
Of neighborhood's extent.
Brothers and sisters, rally forth
To go where we are sent. Amen.

2. Come, Meek of the Earth

Advent 2   *11.11.11.11.*

Come, meek of the earth, from all stations in life.
Let God's promised harmonies end all our strife.
The Chosen One calls from the womb of God's love:
Repent now, to enter the realm from above.

No longer will earth's pomp and glory impress.
While power once charmed us, we now will confess
Our faith in the One whom creation adores,
Whose message is peace that will finish our wars.

Baptize us with fire, and your Spirit bring near
That mercy may free us your message to hear.
Make enemies friends; grant us love, joy, and peace.
Let labors bear fruit and believing increase.

With trust that is childlike, we worship you now.
Together before you in meekness we bow,
Preparing our hearts for the coming of One
Who fills us with hope in salvation begun. Amen.

---

3. "Are You the One?"

Advent 3   *L.M. 8.8.8.8.*

"Are you the One," the Baptist cried,
"With saving grace come to abide
Among God's people far and near,
Their tongues to loose, their cries to hear?"

The deserts blossom, waters spring,
And everlasting gladness bring
To weakened knees and eyes, once blind,
To stopped-up ears and fast-closed mind.

All sorrows flee as we are healed,
The majesty of God revealed.
All grumblings cease and joy sets fire
To songs of praise from pew and choir. Amen.

---

4. Emmanuel Is Drawing Near

Advent 4   *C.M. 8.6.8.6.*

Emmanuel is drawing near,
The signs are all around.
The perfect love that casts out fear
Breaks forth in every sound.

Behold, a virgin shall conceive
And bear God's human child.
Both poor and mighty shall believe
One pure and undefiled.

The child shall reign with truth and grace,
Salvation to reveal,
Our doubts and questions to erase,
All hurt and sin to heal.

Once more God calls, our faith renews,
And summons us to care.
Good over evil, you shall choose
And God's peace you shall share. Amen.

---

5. A Dark, Expectant, Waiting World
MARY JACKSON CATHEY, 1977

Advent/Christmas   *C.M.D. 8.6.8.6.D*

A dark, expectant, waiting world
Lay dormant in the night,
The promise of the ages gone
Foretold a saving light.
All eyes looked for the promised sign,
A star to show the way;
All ears alert to angels' song
To welcome a new day.

In joy and hope our days are spent
The coming to proclaim;
That all may share the glorious love
And wonders of Christ's name.
Arise, sing out! Our Lord has come;
The hallelujah sounds,
Emmanuel means God with us
And love that knows no bounds.

God grant us grace to share your light
That shines for all to see;
Salvation is your wondrous gift

Of love both pure and free.
Now send us forth to do your work,
The Christ event to tell;
Our Lord has come, Messiah reigns!
All praise Emmanuel! Amen.

Hymns for the Christmas Season

6. Light Dispels the Shadows

Christmas Eve/Day   8.7.8.7.8.7.

Light dispels the shadows 'round us;
Hear from Bethlehem, good news.
In a baby, God has found us,
Calls us back, love's way to choose.
Light of Lights, our way illumine;
Grant us peace, forgive our sin.

We rejoice at words of promise,
Meant for all who feel oppressed.
Earth's injustice and unfairness,
All that's wrong, will be redressed.
Light of Lights, our way illumine;
Grant us peace, forgive our sin.

Yokes are broken, freedom granted,
Worldly passions overcome.
Hallelujahs still are chanted;
God's work is not burdensome.
Light of Lights, our way illumine;
Grant us peace, forgive our sin.

Chosen people, live for others;
Share the good news everywhere.
One at heart, sisters and brothers,
Fling God's songs into the air.
Light of Lights, our way illumine;
Grant us peace, forgive our sin. Amen.

7. Trumpets and Voices

Trumpets and voices, bright skies and great joy:
Heav'ns celebrations no gloom can destroy.
Come to the manger, kneel in awe and praise;
Let God's salvation transform all your days.

Prepare the way for peace amid our fears.
Rejoice as hope, once hid, now reappears.
God's holy people, justified by grace,
Moved by a manger, can a cross embrace.

Fired by the wonder of this humble birth,
We reaffirm each person's sacred worth.
Saved not by deeds, but by God's mercy spared,
We seek to share with all our Savior's care. Amen.

8. A Light Shines in the Darkness

A light shines in the darkness;
The Word-made-flesh has come.
The God who led our parents
Now calls us to become
The bearers of good tidings,
Salvation to proclaim,
To people of all nations
Whom God calls out by name.

God spoke in mighty cadence
To ancestors of old.
Now, in a child, the Word comes
In accents clear and bold.
The simple trust of childhood
Declares to all God's reign

And charges us to witness
That earth is God's domain.

Where God rules there is singing
And comfort for the poor.
The trials of earth are lifted
As we learn to endure.
How beautiful on mountains
Are feet that carry truth,
That life is meant for service,
And love restores our youth. Amen.

---

9. Come to the Manger
DAVID E. WILLIAMS

Christmas, Communion   10.10.10.10.

Come to the manger where the Christ Child lay,
Wrapped in his swaddling bands, upon the hay.
Hear, as the angels sing their heav'nly song;
Come, let your heart and soul to him belong.

Come to the hilltop on that darkest day.
See how he takes the cross, our death to slay.
See him arise to free us from our wrong.
Come, let your heart and soul to him belong.

Come to his table as he breaks the bread,
Pours out the cup that we may all be fed.
Come, to the feast of his disciple-throng.
Come, let your heart and soul to him belong. Amen.

---

10. Children of God

Christmas Season   C.M. 8.6.8.6.

Children of God, your light has come,
Adoption is complete.

You are in Christ, the Word made flesh,
Set free from all defeat.

You have been carried, lifted up
By God's abiding power,
Redeemed in love and pity for
The church's finest hour.

Come now to build and plant and heal,
For God's own time is here.
A time to laugh and dance and sing,
For love casts out all fear.

How good it is to worship here
The God who bears our pain
And sends us forth, renewed again,
God's justice to proclaim. Amen.

---

11. Come Believers, Sing Your Praises

Christmas Season   8.7.8.7.

Come, believers, sing your praises;
God has called us all by name,
Poured out blessings in the Spirit
Through the babe of Bethlehem.

Jesus, sent to Egypt's exile,
Knows the stranger in our hearts:
Raised in Naz'reth's narrow vision,
Feels the silence fear imparts.

Christ, as head of all creation,
Robes us with the reconciled,
Grants to each a crown of beauty,
Claims each one as God's own child.

Call to hope, our eyes enlightened,
We enlist in Jesus' cause,
Giving thanks for saints around us,
Serving God without applause.

Join in prayer for one another,
Let our faith and love abound.

We are ready to be workers
Anywhere Christ may be found. Amen.

---

12. Jesus the Christ, Who Came to Earth
MARY J. CATHEY, 1986

First Sunday After Christmas   *L.M. 8.8.8.8.*

Jesus the Christ, who came to earth,
In Bethlehem of simple birth,
Was sent to show God's love for all,
To offer hope, to give the call.

Eternal Spirit, offered then
The self in sacrifice to win
A life forever in God's care
For every person everywhere.

High Priest of all of humankind,
Christ's blood has purified, refined,
To lead us where Christ's feet have trod
To serve the everlasting God.

Offspring of God, your glory shines
Beyond all bounds, beyond all times,
Now give your people eyes to see
The life you gave has set us free. Amen.

---

13. God Is the Word
MARY J. CATHEY, 1986

Second Sunday After Christmas   *10.10.10.10.*

God is the Word, the Source of all of life,
God made all things for peace but not for strife,
When all was darkness, God created light,
Light that outshines the shade of day and night.

God sent a bearer to reveal the Gift,
So could all people know and feel the lift
That comes from Jesus' strong and caring hand,
A chance to know and follow God's command.

Christ came to earth in humble, human form
Filled with all truth and grace so full and warm,
Each day brought service and new work began
Living the days obedient to God's plan.

Out of God's fullness, grace has blessed us all,
Jesus, the Christ, who came to give the call,
To serve our Lord and follow in the way
That shall lead forth from night to endless day. Amen.

---

14. God, Our Alpha and Omega

New Year's Day   8.7.8.7.

God, our Alpha and Omega,
Who, for us, makes all things new,
Make your dwelling place among us.
Come in glory; keep us true.

As a new year dawns among us,
Lead us by your steadfast love
To embrace all nations' hungry
With compassion from above.

Help us leave behind the failures
And frustrations of past years.
May we move ahead more boldly
To reach out in spite of fears.

Grant the water of salvation
And the bread of life to all.
May the earth reflect your newness
Granted now to great and small. Amen.

15. O God, We Celebrate

January 1—Jesus and Mary   10.10.10.10

O God, we celebrate your saving power
Given in Jesus for this present hour.
Thankful for Mary's faithfulness, we sing
Our highest praise, with fear and trem-bl-ing.

Nations, be glad; God judges lovingly,
Rules us with justice, blesses equally.
At Jesus' name we pause on bended knee,
Knowing Christ's faithfulness has set us free.

Show us your face within our life today.
Give us your peace and send us on our way
That we may fathom all your love would give,
Welcome salvation everywhere we live.

We would obey, proclaiming we are yours,
Grateful for faith that through the year endures.
Gird us to share good news our eyes have seen.
Let ev'ry tongue confess the Nazarene. Amen.

Hymns for the Epiphany Season

16. Our Hearts Shall Rejoice

Epiphany   11.11.11.11.

Our hearts shall rejoice and our eyes find delight.
God's glory has risen and sharpened our sight.
The shadows of earth have been melted away,
For One is among us who brings a new day.

"Our worship has led us to follow a star
To bring costly treasure from nations afar,"

Said visitors three, as in rev'rence they bowed
To honor the Christ Child, as once they had vowed.

God's blessing empow'rs us to join with the saints
To show forth God's caring, unbowed by complaints
Of people whose vision has not yet been freed
To see God's salvation poured out for their need.

God's message, compelling, invites us to share
Good news of salvation with friends everywhere.
Equipped and emboldened to witness today
We go as disciples to follow God's way. Amen.

---

17. God Takes Us by the Hand

First Sunday After Epiphany—Baptism of Jesus   *S.M.D. 6.6.8.6.D*

God takes us by the hand
To strengthen and to bless.
We enter into covenant
Our answers to express.
In awe before our God
We listen now to hear
The voice of Majesty and Pow'r,
So still and yet so clear.

The Spirit grants us breath
And calls us by our name.
God shows no partiality,
Each one's worth to proclaim.
In that accepting love
Our spirits find release,
And we are freed from anger's pow'r
To share good news of peace.

The past has come to be;
New things are now declared.
The pris'ners find a blest release
And sight with blind is shared:
How wonderful God's works!
God shakes the wilderness.

With flaming fires God's voice ignites
Our joy and faithfulness. Amen.

---

18. O God, Who Names Us Servants

Second Sunday After Epiphany   7.6.7.6.D

O God, who names us servants
And calls us to be saints,
We ask you now to hear us;
Give ear to our complaints.
The miry bogs have claimed us;
Our labor is in vain.
Do not withhold your mercy,
But give relief from pain.

How patiently we've waited
For you to hear our cry.
Then from the pit you draw us,
Raise up and sanctify.
Your steadfast love preserves us
And saving help proclaims;
Your law on hearts is written
And you have named our names.

Our mouths will sing your praises;
Our steps you've made secure.
You multiply your mercies,
Reach out to reassure.
The glad news of deliverance
With all the world we share:
Your faithfulness is awesome;
It reaches everywhere.

Your gifts, O God, are endless;
How wonderful your deeds!
We know that we are chosen
To deal with people's needs.
A light to all the nations,
In Christ we've strength to be,

By grace and peace empowered
To give our energy. Amen.

---

19. Come . . . Quarreling People

Third Sunday After Epiphany 8.7.8.7.8.7.

Come, distraught and quarreling people,
Deep in shadows, gloom, and fear,
Christ is present to confront us:
Steadfast love of God brought near.
Bring the fragments that are broken
That God's healing may be clear.

When oppressors' rods are broken,
When dissension is addressed,
When from party spir't God frees us,
We resolve to give our best.
Follow where the light is shining
That our words might meet life's test.

Preach and teach the gospel story.
Follow Jesus; leave your nets.
Seize the joy of harvest's labor,
Bowing not to tempter's threats.
Linked in judgment, mind, and spirit,
Praise the One who pardons debts. Amen.

---

20. Dear God, We Bring You

Fourth Sunday After Epiphany 8.8.8.8.

Dear God, we bring you our dismay
At evil's grip on earth today.
Amid our lives and all around
Deceit, false pride, and doubt are found.

Your saving acts have rescued us
When we were weak and envious.
Your truth convicts us of our sin
And calls us to new life within.

We plead our case and turn our backs
On wisdom of the world that lacks
A humble spirit, purity,
And hunger for eternity.

O God, transform our views today;
We want to trust and live your way.
O, grant us justice, mercy, peace;
May love abound and faith increase. Amen.

---

21. We Praise You for Your Mercy

Fifth Sunday After Epiphany   7.6.7.6.D

We praise you for your mercy
That shines on us today,
Great God of all who hunger
And long to find your way.
Your righteousness and justice
And generosity
Have broken yokes' oppression
And set your people free.

No ear has heard your wisdom
Nor eye beheld your light
That shines amid our darkness
To set the world aright.
When we seek our own pleasure
While workers are oppressed,
Your kindly grace informs us
We have not met your test.

O God, forgive our failure
To live as you command.
Our fasting has been selfish,
Our acts of sharing bland.

Hymns for the Epiphany Season   149

Oh, answer us, dear Savior;
We'll never be self-made!
We would be firm and trusting,
Steady and unafraid.

As your forgiven sinners
We seek to salt the earth,
Light up the world for Jesus
And then proclaim Christ's worth.
Let prophets reign among us
Who live within your realm,
Make us your faithful servants
No plight can overwhelm. Amen.

---

22. Blessed Are Those

Sixth Sunday After Epiphany 8.7.8.7.

Blessed are those whose way is blameless,
Those who seek with all their heart
To be faithful to God's precepts,
Keep God's law and do their part.

God has given us the choices:
Life and good or death and wrong.
Let our righteousness be truer
Than all others who are strong.

We will walk as God intended
Without jealousy and strife.
Reconciled with fellow workers,
Celebrate the gift of life.

Keep us steadfast in your service,
God of love and faithfulness.
Fix our eyes on your commandments.
Dwell with us, to love and bless. Amen.

23. O Spirit, Dwell Within

Seventh Sunday After Epiphany   7.6.7.6.D

O Spirit, dwell within us,
God's temple called to be.
Our souls wait now in silence
To sing your melody.
This day is Christ's salvation
Renewed within our lives;
Your steadfast love surrounds us
And hope once more arrives.

You are our rock and fortress,
The source of love and pow'r;
We trust your Spirit's leading
Through this, our worship hour,
We join the singing heavens
To claim God's will on earth.
We enter into cov'nant
With you, who gave us birth.

No way can we deceive you
When, thinking ourselves wise,
Our eyes and hands offend you
And actions cover lies.
From depths of self-deception
Deliver us, we pray;
Release us from the prison
Of our own selfish way.

You answer us and help us
When on your name we call;
You satisfy our hunger
When we give you our call.
O, take our days and use them,
Alive forever more,
To build on those foundations
That others laid before. Amen.

24. Great God of All Myst'ry

Great God of all Myst'ry, Creator of Light,
From all that is hidden, we seek now your sight,
That we with your servants our mission may view
And find in our hearts what you want us to do.

Not evil for evil, not tooth for a tooth,
But prayers for each other partake of your truth.
You say: take no vengeance; no grudge shall you bear.
Love both friend and foe, everyone, everywhere.

O God, you reveal the intent of our hearts;
Perfect and empow'r us to make our new starts.
No hate for a neighbor or curse for the blind,
But selfless provision for poor may you find.

Remove from our lives what is false and profane.
Keep us from injustice against those in pain.
O, make us your stewards and help us to be
Trustworthy and growing in fidelity. Amen.

25. We Wait upon the Mountain

We wait upon the mountain
To hear your word anew,
In statutes for our living
That time has proved so true.
But even more in Jesus,
The Word-made-flesh, do we
In dazzling cloud and sunshine
Your awesome glory see.

Our spirits soar within us
To heights before unknown

When we, in you, take refuge
And find our soul's new home.
Christ came in mighty power,
In majesty revealed,
Yet lived among the humble
Who, in Christ's love, were healed.

No sanctuary's safety
Will keep us in the light,
But only in life's valleys
Will worship grant us sight.
O, help us heed the prophets
And tune ourselves to hear
The message you are sending
To hearts weighed down with fear.
Amen.

---

26. Transfiguration Hymn

DAVID E. WILLIAMS

Last Sunday After Epiphany   *8.6.8.6.8.6.*

O Jesus Christ, who took with you
Peter and James and John
To pray upon the mountaintop
While they stood looking on,
May we who follow you today
Be richly blessed as they!

Your mystery surrounded them
Upon that mountain height,
As they beheld your dazzling face,
And clothing bathed in light,
With lawgiver and prophet, too,
Upon your left and right.

The hour was late, their eyes were dim;
'twas hard to keep awake,
But bravely on they struggled still
For their dear Master's sake.
May we who follow you today
Be found as true as they.

The voice that came from out the cloud
Echoed across the vale,
"This is my own beloved One,"
Whose message will not fail.
O Christ, whose face in glory shone,
Make us also your own! Amen.

Hymns for Lent

27. Come, God's Own People

Ash Wednesday   10.10.10.10

Come, God's own people; know yourselves anew.
Walk with the One whose love for you is true.
Welcome salvation in this time and place.
Return with all your heart to know God's grace.

Hearts waken now with fasting, weeping, too.
Let not earth's treasures blind and capture you.
God sends provisions for our daily need;
There is no place in life for selfish greed.

Fast, then, and pray in private piety.
Sound not the trumpet for your charity.
God, who in secret hears your heartfelt prayer,
Rewards the faithful with a parent's care.

Working with God, join Christ in ministry,
Removing barriers that all may be free,
Suffering affliction, hardships, pain, and loss,
Truthful and loving, fearing not the cross. Amen.

28. We Praise You, Our Creator

First Sunday of Lent   7.6.7.6.D

We praise you, our Creator,
Who formed us from the dust,
And breathed into our nostrils
Life's breath and will to trust.
You gave us one another
To form community
And care for all your creatures
In air and land and sea.

But we rebelled against you
And seldom paused to pray,
In sin, preferred our own view
And turned to our own way.
Temptations were compelling,
Material gain our goal,
The thought of fame exciting,
Our dream, a power role.

Mere bread is insufficient,
You shall not tempt your God;
"There's only One to worship,"
Said Jesus, crying aloud.
The Word of God will teach us
And angels bear us up.
To God belongs our service
Around a common cup.

Then let our hearts be joyful,
As in humility
We join with Christ, our Savior,
To serve humanity.
We seek not fame and fortune
But only to be free,
To share life in the Spirit
With all whose needs we see. Amen.

29. Eternal Life Is with Us Now

Second Sunday of Lent   *C.M.8.6.8.6.*

Eternal life is with us now
And we are born anew.
The Spirit's wind will each endow
And teach us what to do.

Go from the country of your birth,
From life's securities,
From all those things that formed your worth,
E'en from your families.

So said our God to Abraham
And Sarah, long ago.
You'll form a nation true to me
And I will help them grow.

And so God's steadfast love today,
Through all our hopes and fears,
Enables us to find the way
To serve God through the years.

In Christ that love is firm and real.
In Christ all life makes sense.
Our hearts are glad, great joy we feel
And humble confidence. Amen.

30. Make a Joyful Noise

Third Sunday of Lent—Psalm 95   *7.6.7.6.D*
(e.g., ST. KEVIN)

Make a joyful noise to God,
Rock of our salvation.
With thanksgiving, we will laud
God, our sure foundation.
In God's hands are depths of earth,

Heights of mountains also.
Sea and land received their birth
In God's oratorio.

Sing your praise, sheep of God's hand,
People of God's pasture.
Bow down, saints of every land,
Lest we meet disaster.
God our Maker bids us come,
On salvation leaning,
Hear God's voice and be not dumb,
Worship and find meaning. Amen.

---

31. Worship God in Truth

Third Sunday of Lent   8.7.8.7.

Worship God in truth and spirit,
Drink of living water now.
Let all needy people hear it:
Christ has torn all barriers down.

Jesus died to save us sinners,
Who by faith are justified,
Weaklings Christ transforms to winners,
Who to God are reconciled.

When we suffer, Christ goes with us,
Teaching how we can endure.
Character and hope are giv'n us,
Love poured out, our hearts made pure.

Harvest fields are spread before us;
God sends us to labor there.
Sing God's love in mighty chorus;
We have firsthand truth to share. Amen.

32. We Who Stumble

Fourth Sunday of Lent   8.7.8.7.8.7.

We who stumble in the darkness
Seek the light of truth today.
God, our Shepherd, take our weakness;
Turn our evil to your way.
Lead us in the paths of right'ness,
Cleanse our souls from sin, we pray.

God, we stand with your anointed,
Healed of vision that was blurred,
Knowing we're by you appointed
To express your living word,
Freed from idols that disjointed,
That your welcome may be heard.

Even death will not dismay us,
For our eyes are opened wide
To receive your great surprises,
Far above all human pride.
Let no fear or sin delay us,
That we may with you abide. Amen.

33. O God, We Come

Fifth Sunday of Lent   8.8.8.8.

O God, we come in our despair.
Destructive forces fill the air.
Death and decay on ev'ry hand
Dry up our bones, lay waste the land.

Will these bones live and spir'ts revive?
Can we, O God, be made alive?
Address our dullness with your light;
Bring life from death, hope from our fright.

Come, breath of God, with cleansing pow'r.
Dwell in and 'round us in this hour.
Release our minds from hostile flesh,
Uplift our spirits and refresh.

God of the living and the dead,
Through resurrection we are led
From sor'w to joy, from strife to peace,
From all our sin to love's release.

With eager longing we embrace
The better world, which by your grace
Is subject to divine commands
And trusted to disciples' hands. Amen.

Hymns for Holy Week

34. Hosanna, Child of David
(A Dialogue to Be Sung Antiphonally)

Palm Sunday   7.6.7.6.D

"Hosanna, Child of David!
Blessed is the Human One
Who comes, salvation bringing
And light, bright as the sun."
"O, save your coats and branches;
This little fad will pass,
Who is this riding by us
On humble, borrowed ass?"

"A prophet, come from Naz'reth
Who showed us God is love.
In Jesus we've a Savior,
Sent here from God above."
"How can a servant save us?
Shall one so humble reign?
We see no signs of mast'ry;
That one will suffer pain!"

"God's pow'r is not in armies
Or honors carved in stone.
In simple care for others,
In giving, there's a throne."
**"What strange ideas possess you!
These people must be mad!
Yet happiness seems genuine;
This One has made them glad!"**

"O, wave your branches with us.
Our Sovereign One is here;
This Jesus is Messiah,
Eternal God brought near."
**"Your ardor is compelling,
Your witness provident,
Your love and kindness augur
Life that is different."**

(All together)
Hosanna, Child of David!
Blessed is the Human One!
God's love has dawned among us,
A better day begun.
Our praise and thanks we offer,
Fresh hymns of joy we sing.
This day the world shall know the
Commitment that we bring. Amen.

---

35. God Wakens Us Today

Passion Sunday   S.M.6.6.8.6.

God wakens us today
From brokenness and grief.
From dread and mis'ry on our way,
God promises relief.

The Christ, who emptied self
And yielded life for all,
Who turned away from fame and wealth
Delivers God's great call.

We, who cried, "Crucify,"
And washed our hands of blame,
Have been forgiv'n 'though we deny
The pow'r of Jesus' name.

Christ saves with steadfast love,
As one who would not grasp
Equality with God above,
Was faithful to the last.

Open our eyes to see
That face so shining bright
Which welcomes us to ministry
And bathes our souls in light. Amen.

---

36. Our God Created
MARY J. CATHEY, 1986

Monday of Holy Week   *C.M.8.6.8.6.*

Our God created all of life
With humankind the prize,
Then sent to earth the only Son
To teach and to baptize.

Our God sent Jesus to this earth
To help us followers be,
To show us love and reverence,
To set all people free.

Our God is faithful, just, and wise,
Dependable, secure,
Through all the ages God has stood
To make the Word endure.

Our God has shown in every age
The greatness and the care
Surrounding every act of life;
We know God's always there. Amen.

37. Hear Now Our Prayer, O Lord
MARY J. CATHEY, 1986

Tuesday of Holy Week 10.10.10.10.

Hear now our prayer, O Lord, we make to you,
Keep and direct us all life's journey through,
Safe in your wisdom, guided by your power,
Trusting your presence each and every hour.

Hear, Sovereign Lord, as we accept your grace,
Rescued and sheltered in a special place,
Protect, defend us in the days ahead
That we may follow where your steps have led.

Hear, Great Jehovah, tributes that we bring,
As, bowed in worship, to our God we sing.
Chosen, appointed, saved to do your will
May we now serve you and your plan fulfill. Amen.

38. Lord, Who Is It?
MARY JACKSON CATHEY, 1986

Wednesday of Holy Week 7.6.7.6.D

"Lord, who is it?" they asked him,
Disciples of his day,
As Jesus sat at table
With followers of his way.
They looked at one another
In quiet disbelief
With many questions forming
No answer brought relief.

"Lord, who is it?" they asked him
And looked at those around,
They sought to understand him
An answer to be found.
Our Jesus knew betrayal

But stood steadfast and strong,
His time was coming quickly
His days would not be long.

"Lord, who is it?" they questioned,
The followers sought to know
The name of the offender
Who troubled Jesus so.
In quiet resignation
Our Lord received the sign
That Judas used to show him,
Betrayal by design.

Disciples thought and questioned
The meaning of Christ's death,
They saw the awful suffering,
They heard the final breath.
But on that darkened hillside
From death new life was born,
The gift of life eternal,
A resurrection morn. Amen.

---

39. This Solemn Night

Maundy Thursday   *L.M.8.8.8.8.*

This solemn night we bow in prayer
In grateful mem'ry of your care,
Shown in the One from Galilee,
Whose table draws us close to thee.

We hear Christ's word, "Remember me,"
And in these moments bow the knee
In awe and gratitude before
The One whom earth and heav'n adore.

For us, Christ took a servant's role,
Washing our feet to make us whole,
Off'ring the cup and breaking bread,
That fearful spirits might be fed.

Let not divisions mar this feast

Nor selfish motives be unleashed.
We seek salvation's unity
As covenanting family.

"Love one another," Jesus said,
As to the cross he looked ahead.
Wash others' feet, wipe tears from eyes.
Turn stumbling ones toward God's surprise. Amen.

---

40. O Day of Sad Remembrance

Good Friday   *7.6.7.6.D*

O day of sad remembrance,
Of suff'ring, pain, and death.
How shall we face the horror
Of Jesus' ebbing breath?
Despised, rejected, broken,
Christ haunts our memory
Of times that our denial
Have hung him on the tree.

When Christ, to truth, bore witness,
We could not find a place
To let that truth find lodging
Within our daily pace.
Obedient through suff'ring,
Christ led the way for us.
But we, like Peter, opt for
A course less perilous.

O, why have we forsaken
The One who loved so much?
Why strayed we from the Shepherd
And from the caring touch
Of One whose welcome reckoned
No partiality,
But met each sister, brother
In warm equality?

O God, we cry for answers
When, by our sin depressed,

We feel poured out like water
And we are sore distressed.
"Our bones are out of joint" and
"Our strength is all dried up,"
But Christ renews the offer
Of healing bread and cup. Amen.

---

41. My God, My God
MARY JACKSON CATHEY, 1986

Good Friday   C.M.8.6.8.6.

"My God, my God" came Jesus' cry
With agonizing voice
In pain and tears the plea arose
For God to make a choice.

"My God, my God," our Jesus prayed
While hanging on the cross.
In calm obedience took the same;
The world sustained the loss.

"My God, my God," the words rang out
With suff'ring and with tears.
This act of dying for our sins
Has quieted all fears.

"My God, my God," upon that cross
The Human One did die,
But God's own child rose up again
Eternal life to buy.

"My God, my God," as followers true,
Let us approach the throne,
For mercy, grace, and total love
The suffering act has shown.

"My God, my God," we pray to you,
High Priest of all our lives.
Salvation is for everyone
Who in your life survives. Amen.

Hymns for the Easter Season

42. We Come to You, Rejoicing

Easter Sunday   7.6.7.6.D

We come to you, rejoicing,
O Maker of our days.
We sing glad songs of vict'ry
To welcome Christ with praise.
The bonds of death no longer
Hold one who came to save,
For Christ, who reigns among us,
Has triumphed o'er the grave.

We join the great thanksgiving
Of Mary at the tomb,
Amazed at your surprises
That cancel fear and gloom.
We know Christ present with us;
The stone is rolled away
And barriers we've created
Can't stand on this new day.

The Risen One among us
Says: "Seek the things above.
Put now to death the earthly
That you may know God's love.
No anger, lies, and malice
Shall have a place within."
O God, remove them from us
And take away our sin.

Renewed in God's own image,
We sing our Maker's praise.
Forgiv'n and healed, we witness
With hearts now set ablaze
To share good news with others,
To preach and testify
That Christ has given purpose
To all beneath the sky. Amen.

43. Celebrate with Joy and Singing
MARY J. CATHEY, 1986

Easter Sunday (Alternate Reading)   8.7.8.7.D

Celebrate with joy and singing,
Alleluia be our song.
Jesus Christ has risen to save us,
Praises to our Christ belong.
Through great love has come the victory;
Life, not death, can be our claim.
Let us now declare Christ's greatness,
Spread good news, proclaim Christ's name.

Honor, glory, praise, thanksgiving
Give we now to God above.
With the cross and grave Christ bought us,
Let us now return that love.
By our lives of dedication,
As we teach and testify,
May we show Christ's love around us,
May it grow and purify.

Worship now with shouts of gladness,
For the Christ, the Holy One,
On this day of resurrection,
For the world new life has won.
Let us pray and praise the Savior,
Trust the acts, believe the word.
Our salvation has been purchased
By our loving, Risen Lord. Amen.

44. Rejoice, All People

Second Sunday of Easter   10.10.10.10.

Rejoice, all people; let our hearts be glad.
Hopes, born anew, are in salvation clad.

Revive our spirits, test our faith by fire.
O God, be with us and our lives inspire.

Receive the Holy Spirit and forgive
All who offend you, that your soul may live.
In Christ receive a goodly heritage.
Love and believe, and all of life engage.

We dwell secure with you, O God, to guide.
Help us to use the gifts that you provide.
Instruct our hearts that we, in turn, may serve
In trials or gladness with new faith and verve.

Show us the paths on which your saints have trod.
Make known your way; direct our steps, O God.
Send us to witness to the peace Christ brings.
As earth rejoices and all heaven sings. Amen.

---

45. Open Your Eyes and See

Third Sunday of Easter   S.M.D.6.6.8.6.D

Open your eyes and see
That Christ is present here,
A prophet strong in word and deed
Who taught us not to fear.
Alive with us to stay,
On walks or breaking bread,
The Sovereign Jesus promises
We will be loved and fed.

May we be born anew
By your abiding word
To serve the truth with gen'rous hearts,
And may our thanks be heard.
Your bounty we enjoy;
Your praises we would sing.
O, purify our souls within,
That others we may bring.

Live in community
With all whom Christ forgave.

Let people, more than things we own,
Be what we seek to save.
Uphold each one in prayer
And give to those in need,
Believers struggling side by side
To serve in word and deed. Amen.

---

46. Gentle Shepherd, Lead Today
(Based on Psalm 23)

Fourth Sunday of Easter   *7.7.7.7.*

Gentle Shepherd, lead today.
We would follow all the way:
In your company be seen,
Stop to rest in pastures green.

Lead beside the waters still
As we seek to do your will.
Day by day our souls restore,
Lead in righteous paths once more.

When we walk through death's dark vale,
Your assurance will not fail.
Then no evil shall we fear
When your rod and staff are near.

When our enemies surround
At your table we are found.
Your anointing touch we know
And with joy our cups o'erflow.

All our lives your goodness flows;
Where we are, your mercy goes.
In your love we will do well.
Lead us home, with you to dwell. Amen.

47. Christ Is the Way

Fifth Sunday of Easter　　　　　　　　　　　　　　　　8.8.8.8.

Christ is the way, the truth, the life,
Who came to earth to share God's plan,
To show God's glory everywhere,
In every age since time began.

In Christ we know we're chosen ones
Whom God delivers from their sins
And calls to tell the wondrous deeds
Through which God loves and disciplines.

Incline your ear, O gracious God;
Be our strong fortress, lest we fail
To put away pretense and guile
And, by default, let wrong prevail.

The greater works Christ bids us do
Await us now on ev'ry hand.
Equip us, God, as we commit
Our way to follow your command. Amen.

48. Bless God, All You People

Sixth Sunday of Easter　　　　　　　　　　　　　　　*11.11.11.11.*

Bless God, all you people, and sing out your praise,
For God has supported us through all our days.
Through trial and testing we've made our defense
And lived by our vows with a strong confidence.

The Maker of all worlds transcends human shrines,
Yet, to humankind, list'ning ear still inclines.
God bids us repent and is anxious to save,
With love that is steadfast through death and the grave.

When suff'ring for righteousness' sake, we will know
God's care will continue and not let us go.

To all who oppress us and God's word deny,
With rev'rence and gentleness we will reply.

From God comes all being, all movement, all life.
We live in the Spirit, in peace and in strife.
To those for whom God is as yet an unknown,
We tell of the hope that within us has grown. Amen.

---

49. Clap Your Hands for Joy
MARY JACKSON CATHEY, 1986

Ascension Day   *8.7.8.7.8.7.*

Clap your hands for joy, all people
Join the followers, join the throngs.
Jesus Christ has given the victory;
To believers it belongs.
Praise to Christ for our salvation,
Glorify Christ's name with songs.

Sound the trumpets, clang the cymbals,
Tell the news out loud and clear:
Jesus Christ has loved and chosen
All who come from far and near.
Promise of the Holy Spirit
Into every life is here.

Shout the message, tell the story
Of our God's revealing gift.
Christ will bless and give us wisdom,
Grant us grace and power swift.
We, the church, Christ's earthly body,
Love and praises now do lift. Amen.

50. Sing Praises and Be Joyful

Seventh Sunday of Easter   7.6.7.6.D

Sing praises and be joyful;
God dwells with us today.
The desolate find meaning
Amid life's disarray.
Bereaved, whom losses cripple,
Are comforted and blessed.
The homeless find a dwelling;
The weary know God's rest.

God's Spirit comes upon us,
Who share Christ's suffering.
Anxiety is tempered
And fear is lessening.
The Holy Spirit's power
Is sent to set us free
To witness to all nations
God's gracious charity.

Through earthquake, rain, and evil
Our faith continues strong.
God will restore, establish,
And bless our lives with song.
Through wilderness and trial
We turn to God in prayer.
Our humble search God blesses
With life beyond compare.

O, keep us near to Jesus,
Who lived your will on earth,
Whose every thought and action
Led folks to claim their worth.
Eternal life is in us,
God's truth unfolds each day.
Be sober, watchful, caring,
Rejoicing, come what may, Amen.

Hymns for the Pentecost Season

51. Spirit of God, Revive

Pentecost   *S.M.D.6.6.8.6.D*

Spirit of God, revive
All souls weighed down with care.
Creator of the universe,
Go with us everywhere.
Our Rock of certainty,
Fresh rain on thirsty land,
Bring wind and fire and confidence
To those whom you command.

We look to you for food,
For body, mind, and soul.
And when your hand is opened wide
We find ourselves made whole.
How manifold your works,
In wisdom shared with all;
O, may we dream and prophesy
In answer to your call.

We sing to you, O God,
As long as we shall live
And go with Christ where we are sent
To witness and forgive.
Amazing God, may we,
By Holy Spir't prepared,
Pour out upon all flesh the love
Christ's actions have declared. Amen.

---

52. The Spirit Among Us
DAVID E. WILLIAMS

Pentecost Season   *11.11.11.11.*

The Spirit among us now calls us to love
As Christ loved the needy when sent from above,

For we are God's people, and all called to be
God's servants, God's children, God's own family.

The Spirit among us now calls us to live
With hearts full of patience and will to forgive,
For we are God's people and gathered to be
Christ's sisters and brothers, in one family.

The Spirit of Jesus now fills us with pow'r.
To know love and peace, e'en in life's darkest hour.
We will be Christ's people and sing of God's grace
Until our dear Savior we meet face to face.

O Spirit among us, stay near us we pray,
A light to our footsteps through each passing day;
Keep each of us faithful in cov'nant with you:
Your servants, your children, your family true. Amen.

---

53. In Awe, We Come to Worship

Trinity Sunday   7.6.7.6.D

In awe, we come to worship
The Three-in-One made known.
By Word we were created,
By steadfast Love, we've grown.
The Word-made-flesh in Jesus
Has taught and healed us all.
The Holy Spirit quickens
Our hearts to heed God's call.

With harp and song, our voices
Rejoice in God and praise
The good news of deliv'rance
That sets our hearts ablaze.
With righteousness and justice,
God frees us all to be
Disciples who are serving
With Christ, eternally.

Now, by your grace improving,

O God, we face the test.
We feel your Spirit's movement
And act at your behest
To share in truth and goodness
The peace Christ came to give,
Agreeing with each other
That by your love we'll live. Amen.

---

54. Venture, All People

Second Sunday After Pentecost   C.M.8.6.8.6.

Venture, all people, where God leads.
Trust that God will provide.
Know our Creator meets our needs
And will be near to guide.

Not everyone who calls on God
Serves with integrity.
False prophets come where Christ has trod
With double-hearted plea.

People who serve, their God to please,
May suffer disrepute.
Good fruit will come from healthy trees;
Bad trees bear evil fruit.

We will not boast of our good deeds,
As if they justified
For, in God's grace, a sinner needs
Faith in Christ, crucified.

How can we build upon a rock
Where some have built on sand?
Listen to Christ, while others mock;
Follow, and understand. Amen.

55. Amid Our Fears

Third Sunday After Pentecost   L.M.8.8.8.8.

Amid our fears we seek your face,
O God of love and pow'r and grace.
In pain we feel so far away
From those who follow in your way.

We bear great sorrow in our hearts
And need the comfort Christ imparts.
We seek the Great Physician's face,
All wrong within us to erase. ·

O God, you bring new life from death,
To stumbling ones give second breath.
In darkest hours you strength provide,
Keep us alert and open-eyed.

The gen'rous gifts your love imparts
Call forth response within our hearts.
As Jesus bids us, "Follow me,"
We seek to live inclusively. Amen.

56. God Is Our Refuge

Fourth Sunday After Pentecost   L.M.8.8.8.8.

God is our refuge and our strength,
Through all life's width and breadth and length.
We will not fear as mountains shake;
God will prevail, all weapons break.

Create a stillness in our hearts
To know the gifts your love imparts.
May we be quiet for a while;
Come now, in Christ, to reconcile.

May Christ's forgiving love empower
The giving of our best this hour,

That Christ's compassion we may share
And by our deeds good news declare.

"To heal the sick and raise the dead
Is our commission," Jesus said.
The realm of God is now at hand;
Be laborers, at Christ's command. Amen.

---

57. Surely, Our God Is in This Place

Fifth Sunday After Pentecost　　　　　　　　　　C.M.8.6.8.6.

Surely, our God is in this place.
We will not fear the dark.
Night holds no terror when we know
Its arrows will miss the mark.

We trust our God who promises:
"I'll keep you 'e'er you go."
Forgiveness comes as God's free gift
That we will ne'er outgrow.

God's house is called the gate of heav'n.
It's here we know God's realm.
This refuge gives us confidence
No foe can overwhelm.

We seek to serve as we've been taught
And let the Spirit speak
Within our lives, as we proclaim
Good news to strong and weak. Amen.

---

58. Be with Us, God

Sixth Sunday After Pentecost　　　　　　　　　　7.6.7.6.D

Be with us, God, to bless us,
For we have wrestled hard

To find the truth within us
We cannot disregard.
Your steadfast love has tested
Our credibility,
And we have followed bravely
In honest loyalty.

We've left our sin behind us
To follow in your path,
And you have walked there with us,
Protecting us from wrath
Of friends and foes around us,
E'en in our families.
Our love for them is boundless,
But you we must first please.

We take Christ's cross to follow
Where you would have us go.
We risk our lives to find them;
We give that we might grow.
To thirsty ones we offer
Cool water in Christ's name;
To all our sisters, brothers
Your message we proclaim. Amen.

---

59. Defender of All

Seventh Sunday After Pentecost   11.11.11.11.

Defender of all who upon your name call,
We ask for your help lest we stumble and fall.
Our enemies threaten us on ev'ry hand.
O, come to support us and help us to stand.

O Maker of heaven and earth, hear our prayer
And rescue us when we are caught in a snare.
There's evil inside us we don't understand
And good we intend that does not go as planned.

When sin dwells within us, we long to be free,
Find rescue and pardon and go on to be

Disciples and prophets, alive with your word,
Proclaiming and living the truth we have heard.

When burdened and weak, beaten down and depressed,
We turn to the One who has promised us rest.
As others have learned when the gentle Christ spoke,
Our souls, now refreshed, can take Christ's easy yoke. Amen.

---

60. O God, to Whom

Eighth Sunday After Pentecost   *10.10.10.10.*

O God, to whom no one is foreigner,
No one disowned, whatever may occur,
We come like strangers to this house of prayer,
Feeling alone, yet still within your care.

Let those who hope in you be saved from shame,
And all who seek to honor Jesus' name
Find no reproach, but rise above cruel scorn
To righteousness, through steadfast love reborn.

Ashes and fasting do not meet our goals
When foul discouragement weighs down our souls,
When we are overwhelmed and need a friend,
You come to us to rescue and defend.

Freed from past slav'ry, we will now survive;
Claimed as your own, we now can come alive.
Your faithful help has set us in your way,
Filled with the Spirit for your own new day. Amen.

---

61. Spirit of Christ Who Gives
MARY JACKSON CATHEY, 1986

Eighth Sunday After Pentecost   *L.M.8.8.8.8.*

Spirit of Christ who gives us life,
Grant now a vision for the soul,

Show us the way to serve in love,
That tempers us and makes us whole.

Spirit of life that moves in all,
Fill us with zeal to follow now,
Give us the word of hope to share
That all may hear and all may bow.

Spirit of God, we claim your gift,
The promise of your saving grace,
Your suffering, death, and glory show
A love that shall the world embrace. Amen.

---

62. O God, Our Souls Are Grateful

Ninth Sunday After Pentecost   7.6.7.6.D

O God, our souls are grateful
For all your benefits.
You heal disease, forgive us,
And bear our deficits.
Your graciousness and mercy
Are filled with steadfast love.
Your pity for your children
Is high as heaven above.

You pull us from the depth of
Our deepest life's despair
And give us wings like eagles'
To follow anywhere.
You pour out good upon us
And send us on our way
Inspired, refreshed, and furnished
To serve without delay.

On holy ground we're standing;
That ground is everywhere.
Throughout your good creation
Your Spirit helps us care
For hungry ones and thirsty,
For pris'ners locked in fear,

For lost and stumbling brothers
And sisters Christ holds dear.

O God of burning bushes,
Give us the eyes to see
Your love at work among us
In common ministry.
Set us aflame with passion
To set your people free,
To break the chains that bind us
And foster harmony. Amen.

---

63. Give Thanks to God

Tenth Sunday After Pentecost   *L.M.8.8.8.8.*

Give thanks to God with all your hearts
For all the treasure God imparts.
Tell of God's wondrous works today.
Sing praises all along your way.

Call on God's name that all may know
The source of strength that helps us grow.
Know that God's covenant is power.
Live in God's presence hour by hour.

Seek God, rejoicing, and declare
God's glory now in earnest prayer.
With those who love as Christians should,
God works in everything for good.

With all God's saints, we seek the best
And give our all as we've been blessed.
When, in our weakness, courage fails,
God's interceding Spir't prevails.

That Spirit searches hearts devout
With sighs too deep for words to shout.
All whom God calls are justified
And in God's image glorified. Amen.

64. At the Feet of Jesus

Eleventh Sunday After Pentecost   6.5.6.5.D *with refrain (11.11.11.11.11.11.)*
(e.g., ST. GERTRUDE)

At the feet of Jesus, we have met to learn.
Here we feel Christ's presence each time we return
We are fed through sharing what each has to give,
Thanking Christ who blesses those who want to live.
Present, past, or future, height or depth or sod
Shall not separate us from the love of God.

Steadfast in the morning, God delivers us,
Brings us out of trouble in new exodus,
With Christ's interceding, spirits will be strong:
We are more than conq'rors and to Christ belong.
Present, past, or future, height or depth or sod
Shall not separate us from the love of God.

Hear our prayer, Creator, in your faithfulness.
Thirsty souls are panting in our eagerness
To be raised with Jesus, your new way to go.
Grant us strength and courage while we dwell below.
Present, past, or future, height or depth or sod
Shall not separate us from the love of God. Amen.

65. God of Cloud and Burning Fire

Twelfth Sunday After Pentecost   7.7.7.7.

God of cloud and burning fire,
Fill us with a strong desire
To be witnesses today
To your loving, better way.

We would praise your wondrous work
And, in faith, would never shirk
Promised vows we've made to you,
To your covenant be true.

When we see Christ pray alone,
We our sin confess and own,
Seeking amnesty once more.
Grant assurance, we implore.

Save us from our baseless fears.
Keep us growing through the years.
Strengthen love, make faith more sure.
Stay with us and keep us pure. Amen.

---

66. Give Ear to All God Teaches

Thirteenth Sunday After Pentecost   *7.6.7.6.D*

Give ear to all God teaches;
Hear what our forebears knew.
God led through desert wand'rings
With cloud and light in view.
Great God, we have forgotten
The care that you endow.
Recall in us your covenant;
Have mercy on us now.

Give voice to God's intention
That all the world may hear:
In Christ we're offered wholeness
To overcome all fear.
Great God, awaken in us
A faith to match our vow
To serve you in each moment;
Have mercy on us now.

Give heart and soul to mission,
That other folks may live.
May holiness enliven
Our passion to forgive
The wrongs that we have suffered
And evil we allow,
Great God of endless kindness,
Have mercy on us now. Amen.

67. Come, Let Us Sing to God

Fourteenth Sunday After Pentecost   S.M.6.6.8.6. (*or as 3 verses—S.M.D.*)

Come, let us sing to God
With joyous songs of praise.
The Rock of our salvation, laud
And bless through all our days.

We worship and bow down
And give you thanks today
For depths of earth and mountain heights
And hearing when we pray.

Keep us from burdened hearts
That proof and safety seek.
We listen for your voice of truth
When we are strong or weak.

Your wisdom runs so deep
That, in your Mystery,
We're awed and silenced, lest we speak
In utter blasphemy.

In Christ we've seen your face.
In Christ we dare confess
The faith that in us lies so deep
That we can scarce express.

We kneel in Jesus' name
To call him Christ and Lord.
The Sovereign Leader of the earth,
Be faithfully adored! Amen.

68. All That Our God Has Spoken

Fifteenth Sunday After Pentecost   *10.10.10.10.*

All that our God has spoken we will do:
Obey God's voice, to covenant be true.

God bears us up on eagle's soaring wing
As mountains tremble and hills skip and sing.

Be not conformed to standards of the world;
Look up to see God's perfect will unfurled.
Judge not yourself more highly than you ought,
But dare to sacrifice as Christ has taught.

In self-denial Jesus chose the cross
And bids us follow, risking pain and loss,
Finding our life beyond the fear of death,
Worshiping with our all while God gives breath.

Called out by Christ to teach and serve with zeal,
We would, to others, carry God's appeal,
With love and cheerfulness, God's mercy show
And give the best we have where'er we go. Amen.

---

69. Glory Be to Our Creator

Sixteenth Sunday After Pentecost 8.7.8.7.

Glory be to our Creator,
Who above the heavens reigns,
Blesses all, both small and mighty,
And our mutual love ordains.

We are made to help each other
And to dwell in harmony.
When relationships are broken,
God provides agreement's key.

Talk about what is between you;
Listen that you both may hear.
Let some other stand beside you
Helping both to make things clear.

Let the church be reconciler,
When we gather, two or three,
God is present and will bless us
With a greater clarity.

Love of self and love of neighbor
Summarize our God's commands.

Each is valued by our Savior,
And by each of us Christ stands.

Glory be to our Creator,
Who has raised us from the dust.
We will turn from all our idols
And give God our love and trust. Amen.

---

70. O Rock and Redeemer

Seventeenth Sunday After Pentecost   *11.11.11.11.*

O Rock and Redeemer, accept from the start
The words of my mouth and the thoughts of my heart.
Wipe out all the arrogant sins from my soul;
Of hidden faults clear me and then make me whole.

As you have forgiven, so may we forgive.
Unlimited mercy has helped us to live
In gen'rous response to our neighbors in need,
Not waiting to see if they're "worthy" in deed.

You rescued a people from bondage and sin
And gave them commandments to cleanse them within.
In love that is steadfast, you said, "Do not fear,
For those who obey, I will make all things clear."

We follow the sabbath to honor you, God;
May worship equip us to go where Christ trod.
We live not to self but that Jesus may reign,
Not judging, but trusting that we'll live again. Amen.

---

71. We Live Today

Eighteenth Sunday After Pentecost   *L.M.8.8.8.8.*

We live today in Jesus Christ,
Who is the way, the truth, the life.

Risking our all, for death is gain,
We face, with courage, ev'ry strife.

We live today within God's grace
And steadfast love, which makes us strong
To turn from idols we have made,
That God may burn away our wrong.

We live today in prayer and praise
For our deliv'rance from God's wrath.
Filled with the fruit of righteousness,
We will pursue our Savior's path.

We live today in boundless joy,
Seeking to show the gospel's pow'r,
Reaching for what is excellent
In ev'ry circumstance and hour. Amen.

---

72. God Reigns!

Nineteenth Sunday After Pentecost   *S.M.6.6.8.6.*

God reigns! All people quake,
For God, exalted, rules
O'er all the reach of time and space,
O'er gifted ones and fools.

Our God has lifted Christ
Above our human scene,
That knees might bow and tongues confess
The Sov'reign Christ, serene.

Let all partake of joy
Who share the mind of Christ,
Who empty self of all those things
That Jesus sacrificed.

Serve in humility
As you have said you would.
May God and people count on you
To go on doing good.

God's mercy will attend
Us on our homeward way:

Work out your own salvation, and
The call of God obey. Amen.

---

73. Sing the Praise of God

Twentieth Sunday After Pentecost   8.7.8.7.D

Sing the praise of God, who loves us,
Blesses us with all good gifts,
Readies us for lives more faithful
To the call that Christ uplifts.
We are servants in God's vineyard,
Planted here to bear good fruit.
May a harvest rich in justice,
With God's peace, be our pursuit.

When God's heir has come among us,
We have killed for our own gain,
Turned away as faithless stewards,
Less than gen'rous and humane.
All that God entrusted to us
We have claimed as our just due.
While a host of sisters, brothers,
Suffer hunger we eschew.

Not for long dare we continue
Enemies of Jesus' cross,
Serving self, rejecting others
As they live with pain and loss.
Christ has set a goal before us
In the upward call of God.
Following that great example,
May we walk where Jesus trod. Amen.

74. Be with Us Here

Twenty-first Sunday After Pentecost   C.M. 8.6.8.6.

Be with us here, O God of peace,
Whose word the winds obey.
O, give our eyes and ears release
To see and hear your way.

Fill ev'ry heart, O God of peace,
With honor, truth, and grace.
May we our love and praise increase
And all Christ's strength embrace.

Attune our lives, O God of peace,
To do the truth we claim.
In wisdom, we would never cease
To honor Jesus' name.

Then send us forth, O God of peace,
To serve where Christ would lead.
And free us from our sins' caprice
To meet another's need. Amen.

75. In Faithful Love Abiding

Twenty-second Sunday After Pentecost   7.6.7.6.D

In faithful love abiding,
We trust you, Gracious God,
So happy in the presence
Of Christ, who this earth trod.
Our prayers of thanks we offer
For all the gospel's pow'r
To turn us from our idols
To serve you in this hour.

You open eyes once blinded
And set the pris'ner free.
Each sojourner, defended,

Is comforted to see
Your justice executed,
The hungry given food,
Discouraged lifted upward
And granted quietude.

In steadfast love we follow
In paths as yet unknown.
Your spirit ne'er forsakes us
Or lets us stand alone.
So, even in affliction,
No duty will we shirk;
As long as we are living
We'll praise you in our work. Amen.

---

76. O Love, Beyond All Knowing

Twenty-third Sunday After Pentecost   7.6.7.6.D

O Love, beyond all knowing,
We bow before your throne.
In awe we seek your favor
And for our sins atone.
We long to love you fully
With heart and mind and soul,
And seek Christ's reign among us
As first and only goal.

Entrusted with the gospel
We want to share good news
And give ourselves for others,
That all of us may choose
The greatest of commandments
To be our common hope.
O God, in you we prosper
And from you learn to cope.

We seek not fame or honors
But people's common good.
We build, with Christ, a friendly
And sharing neighborhood.

O, help us love more fully
As we are loved by you,
That, valuing all people,
We may, to Love, be true. Amen.

77. Our God, You Grant Us Rest

Twenty-fourth Sunday After Pentecost C.M.8.6.8.6.

Our God, you grant us rest and sleep
When we, in anxious toil,
Think everything depends on us,
Who burn the midnight oil.

You nurse us in our deepest need
With loving gentleness.
You watch, with patience, our desire
To prosper and impress.

Forgive, O God, the burdens we
Impose on others' lives,
For even all the good we do
On recognition thrives.

O, help us now to learn from Christ
And quiet witness make,
To humble selves, in thankful trust,
And serve for others' sake. Amen.

78. The Heavens Declare Your Glory

Twenty-fifth Sunday After Pentecost 7.6.7.6.D

The heavens declare your glory
And all creation speaks
Of care in which you keep us
Through all our days and weeks.

We offer our thanksgiving
And pay our vows, Most High,
For all on earth are yours, as
The righteous testify.

We call in times of trouble
For your deliverance
And turn from empty ritual
And meaningless pretense.
Let justice roll like waters
And righteousness descend,
For you would save your people
And hurting ones defend.

Restore in those who grieve now
A hope that will not die,
For Christ arose in vict'ry
And so shall you and I.
We comfort one another
By God's redeeming grace.
We watch and pray, preparing
To meet Christ face to face. Amen.

---

79. O Sovereign God

Twenty-sixth Sunday After Pentecost   *C.M.D.8.6.8.6.D*

O Sovereign God, you give to us
Our lives, in solemn trust,
Our talents and abilities
To use in causes just.
O, may we act with faithfulness,
Your purpose to fulfill,
That it may be our greatest joy
To live and teach your will.

We serve as children of the day,
Empowered by your light.
In all we do we risk for you
Our wealth or widow's mite.
O, keep us steadfast in those tasks
You set before us now,

And may we never fear or hide
The gifts that you endow.

We seek to build up others and
To brighten all their days.
When we observe the good they do,
We compliment and praise.
May we, together, share ourselves
For one another's good,
That your salvation may be known
In every neighborhood. Amen.

---

80. Our Shepherd and Our Rescuer

Last Sunday After Pentecost   *C.M.D.8.6.8.6.D*

Our Shepherd and our Rescuer,
O God, we seek your face,
For we have wandered far from truth
And your redeeming grace.
O, bring us back to face ourselves
And judgment that awaits;
Remove from us the selfishness
That warps and separates.

We feel estranged from our best selves
And from the love you give;
We long to know your comfort and
A truer way to live.
You gather us, both strong and weak,
No matter where we've strayed,
And in your full acceptance here
We worship unafraid.

In Christ we see your pow'r to save,
And even death destroy.
O, work your miracles in us
That we may yet enjoy
A life of full commitment to
Your purposes for all.
May friend and stranger know through us
Your love for great and small.

Hymns for the Pentecost Season   193

Abiding in forgiveness and
Your gracious providence,
We turn away from selfish pride
And greed and false pretense.
We offer food and drink and care
To all who are in need
And, in your name, we welcome them
With friendly word and deed. Amen.

---

81. Come, All People, Sing
MARY J. CATHEY, 1986

Thanksgiving   8.7.8.7.D

Come, all people, sing God's praises
As we thankfully rejoice,
For God's goodness and all mercies
Let us lift both hands and voice,
For the glory of the mountains,
For the still seas and the wave, .
For the sunrise and the sunset,
For all blessings that God gave.

Sing glad songs of countless wonders,
Our Creator's name extol,
In the meadows and the valleys
Awesome beauty we behold,
For a land supplied with water,
For the vegetation rare,
For provisions and great bounty,
For God's constant love and care.

Shout with joy and bring due honor
For the gift of God, the Son,
In our lives to be the witness
Of the ever-present One,
Blessed Son, who brought salvation,
Blessed One, who gives the call,
Let us now in glad thanksgiving
Come to God to give our all. Amen.

82. Give Thanks, O Christian People
MARY JACKSON CATHEY, 1984

General Thanksgiving   7.6.7.6.D

Give thanks, O Christian people,
For workers of our day,
Who heed the call to service
And make it their life's way,
To go to feed the hungry,
To tend to those in need,
To work for equal justice,
Till all God's folk are freed.

Give thanks, O Christian people,
For leaders of our years,
Who live to share with others
Our joy when Christ appears;
To teach the ones who seek light,
To guide the faltering feet,
To lead the followers forward
Our living Lord to meet.

Give thanks, O Christian people,
For all who love the Lord,
Who live each day believing
In God's eternal word,
To share Christ's love in living,
To witness with each deed,
To use the talents given,
To plant the gospel seed.

Give thanks, O Christian people,   ˙
For life in fellowship
With all who trust our Savior
Their serving to equip.
To ease another's burdens,
To cope in joy and stress,
To magnify God's message
And Christ's great love confess. Amen.

83. Sing, O Sing Glad Songs
MARY JACKSON CATHEY, 1985

General Hymn of Praise   8.7.8.7.D

Sing, O sing glad songs and praises
To the God whom we adore,
Let the joy and love of service
Be our effort evermore.
Give us ways to spend God's kindness,
Live the message, show God's grace.
May we act as true disciples
In this time and in this place.

Raise, now raise all hands in glory
To our God, who loves us all.
May our deeds confirm the story
Of God's way and of the call.
Create tension in our being,
Act to make our lives convey
Signs of hope, of faith, of meaning
As we learn Christ's perfect way. Amen.

84. Eternal Light, Whose Glorious Gleam
MARY JACKSON CATHEY, 1984

General Hymn of Praise   C.M.8.6.8.6.

Eternal Light, whose glorious gleam
Outshines the moon and sun,
Your aura bright eclipses all
The works your hands have done.

Creator of this spinning sphere,
Who did all persons make,
You gave to us the earthly task
Of your commands to take.

Omniscient One, whom we adore,

Look down on humankind,
As worship fills our lives and days
May we your glory find.

All praise to you, the Living God,
The maker of us all,
Our great desire is showing love
As we before you fall. Amen.

---

85. We Claim the Call
CHRISTINE D. BARTON, 1979

Ordination and Installation   8.8.8.8.

We claim the call to ministry,
Then ask, "Why have you chosen me?"
Confused, and wishing to be free.
Lord, hear our cry. Lord, hear our cry.

The doubts we harbor grind us down.
Through search for self we lose our ground.
A fool for Christ turns into clown.
Lord, hear our cry. Lord, hear our cry.

Can we respond to your great call
To take the cup and drink it all?
You seek our wholeness, nothing small.
Lord, hear our cry. Lord, hear our cry.

Now shake our spirits, take our dread.
Give us the will to risk instead
To preach the gospel as Christ said.
Lord, hear our cry. Lord, hear our cry.

Give us the eyes always to see
And share the truth of ministry.
You claim our souls to set us free!
Lord, hear our cry. Lord, hear our cry. Amen.

Indexes

Alphabetical Index of Hymns

Metrical Index of Hymns

Topical Index of Hymns

Our God, You Grant Us Rest   77
Sing Praises and Be Joyful   50

ASSURANCE

Gentle Shepherd, Lead Today   46
Give Thanks to God   63
O Day of Sad Remembrance   40
Our God Created   36
Sing Praises and Be Joyful   50
We Who Stumble   32

CHRISTMAS

A Dark, Expectant, Waiting World   5
A Light Shines in the Darkness   8
Children of God   10
Come, Believers, Sing Your Praises   11
Come to the Manger   9
God Is the Word   13
Jesus the Christ, Who Came to
    Earth   12
Light Dispels the Shadows   6
O God, We Celebrate   15
Trumpets and Voices   7

CHURCH

Children of God   10
Clap Your Hands for Joy   49
Glory Be to Our Creator   69
O Love, Beyond All Knowing   76

COMFORT

A Light Shines in the Darkness   8
Amid Our Fears   55
God Is Our Refuge   56
Our God, You Grant Us Rest   77
Our Shepherd and Our Rescuer   80
Sing Praises and Be Joyful   50
The Heavens Declare Your Glory   78

COMMUNION

Come to the Manger   9
Gentle Shepherd, Lead Today   46
Lord, Who Is It?   38
O Day of Sad Remembrance   40
Open Your Eyes and See   45
This Solemn Night   39
We Claim the Call   85
We Praise You, Our Creator   28

CONFESSION

Amid Our Fears   55
Dear God, We Bring You   20
Defender of All   59
Give Ear to All God Teaches   66
God of Cloud and Burning Fire   65
O Day of Sad Remembrance   40
O Spirit, Dwell Within   23
Our Shepherd and Our Rescuer   80
We Come to You, Rejoicing   42

CONSECRATION AND
DEDICATION

Be with Us, God   58
Celebrate with Joy and Singing   43
Come to the Manger   9
Eternal Life Is with Us Now   29
God of Cloud and Burning Fire   65
In Awe, We Come to Worship   53
Our Shepherd and Our Rescuer   80
Trumpets and Voices   7
We Live Today   71

COURAGE

All That Our God Has Spoken   68
At the Feet of Jesus   64
Be with Us, God   58
Eternal Life Is with Us Now   29
Give Thanks to God   63
God Is Our Refuge   56
Lord, Who Is It?   38
Surely, Our God Is in This Place   57
Venture, All People   54

COVENANT

All That Our God Has Spoken   68
Give Ear to All God Teaches   66
Give Thanks to God   63
God of Cloud and Burning Fire   65
God Takes Us by the Hand   17
O Spirit, Dwell Within   23
The Spirit Among Us   52
This Solemn Night   39

DISCIPLESHIP

Amid Our Fears   55
Be with Us, God   58
Christ Is the Way   47
Defender of All   59
In Awe, We Come to Worship   53

Topical Index of Hymns 203

GOD

Glory of
Come, All People, Sing   81
Eternal Light, Whose Glorious
   Gleam   84
Glory Be to Our Creator   69
Give Thanks to Our God   63
Sing, O Sing Glad Songs   83
Spirit of Christ Who Gives   61
The Heavens Declare Your
   Glory   78
Guidance of
Be with Us, God   58
Be with Us Here   74
Give Ear to All God Teaches   66
God, Our Alpha and Omega   14
In Awe, We Come to Worship   53
O God, Our Souls Are
   Grateful   62
Spirit of God, Revive   51
Venture, All People   54
Love of
A Dark, Expectant, Waiting
   World   5
Amid Our Fears   55
At the Feet of Jesus   64
Emmanuel Is Drawing Near   4
Jesus the Christ, Who Came to
   Earth   12
O God, Our Souls Are
   Grateful   62
O Love, Beyond All Knowing   76
Promise of
A Dark, Expectant, Waiting
   World   5
Come, Meek of the Earth   2
Defender of All   59
Light Dispels the Shadows   6
Surely, Our God Is in This
   Place   57
Providence of
Come, All People, Sing   81
Come, God's Own People   27
Eternal Light, Whose Glorious
   Gleam   84
Gentle Shepherd, Lead Today   46
Give Thanks to God   63
God Is Our Refuge   56
Jesus the Christ, Who Came to
   Earth   12
Make a Joyful Noise   30
O God, to Whom   60
Our God, You Grant Us Rest   77

The Heavens Declare Your
   Glory   78
Reign (Rule) of
A Light Shines in the Darkness   8
Emmanuel Is Drawing Near   4
God Reigns   72
Works of
Eternal Light, Whose Glorious
   Gleam   84
God of Cloud and Burning
   Fire   65
God Takes Us by the Hand   17
In Faithful Love Abiding   75
O God, Our Souls Are
   Grateful   62
Our God Created   36
Sing Praises and Be Joyful   50

GOOD FRIDAY

Come to the Manger   9
God Wakens Us Today   35
O Day of Sad Remembrance   40
O God, We Come   33
This Solemn Night   39
Worship God in Truth   31

GOSPEL

A Dark, Expectant, Waiting World   5
Bless God, All You People   48
Celebrate with Joy and Singing   43
Christ Is the Way   47
Come . . . Quarreling People   19
Give Thanks, O Christian People   82
God Is Our Refuge   56
Light Dispels the Shadows   6
O God, We Celebrate   15
O God, Who Names Us Servants   18
O Love, Beyond All Knowing   76
We Claim the Call   85
We Come to You, Rejoicing   42
We Live Today   71

GRACE

Are You the One?   3
Clap Your Hands for Joy   49
Come, God's Own People   27
God Is the Word   13
Hear Now Our Prayer, O Lord   37
My God, My God   41
Our Shepherd and Our Rescuer   80
Sing, O Sing Glad Songs   83

Spirit of Christ Who Gives   61
Spirit of God, Revive   51
The Spirit Among Us   52

HOPE

A Dark, Expectant, Waiting World   5
Come, Meek of the Earth   2
Dear God, We Bring You   20
O God, to Whom   60
O Love, Beyond All Knowing   76
O Spirit, Dwell Within   23
Rejoice, All People   44
Spirit of Christ Who Gives   61
Spirit of God, Revive   51
Surely, Our God Is in This Place   57
The Heavens Declare Your Glory   78
Worship God in Truth   31

JESUS CHRIST

A Dark, Expectant, Waiting World   5
At the Feet of Jesus   64
Celebrate with Joy and Singing   43
Christ Is the Way   47
Clap Your Hands for Joy   49
Come, Let Us Sing to God   67
Come . . . Quarreling People   19
Give Thanks to God   63
God Is the Word   13
God Reigns   72
God Wakens Us Today   35
Hosanna, Child of David   34
In Awe, We Come to Worship   53
Jesus the Christ, Who Came to
    Earth   12
Lord, Who Is It?   38
My God, My God   41
O Day of Sad Remembrance   40
O God, We Celebrate   15
Open Your Eyes and See   45
Our God Created   36
Sing Praises and Be Joyful   50
This Solemn Night   39
Transfiguration Hymn   26
Trumpets and Voices   7
We Come to You, Rejoicing   42
We Live Today   71
We Wait upon the Mountain   25
Worship God in Truth   31

JOY

A Dark, Expectant, Waiting World   5
Are You the One?   3

Celebrate with Joy and Singing   43
Clap Your Hands for Joy   49
Come, All People, Sing   81
Gentle Shepherd, Lead Today   46
Give Thanks to God   63
God Reigns   72
God Takes Us by the Hand   17
Hosanna, Child of David   34
O Sovereign God   79
Sing, O Sing Glad Songs   83
Sing Praises and Be Joyful   50
Trumpets and Voices   7
We Live Today   71

JUSTICE

Are You the One?   3
Children of God   10
Emmanuel Is Drawing Near   4
Give Thanks to God   63
God, Our Alpha and Omega   14
God Takes Us by the Hand   17
Light Dispels the Shadows   6
O God, Our Souls Are Grateful   62
O God, We Celebrate   15
O God, Who Names Us Servants   18
O Sovereign God   79
Sing the Praise of God   73
The Heavens Declare Your Glory   78
We Praise You, Our Creator   28

LENT

Come, God's Own People   27
Eternal Life Is with Us Now   29
God Wakens Us Today   35
Hear Now Our Prayer, O Lord   37
Hosanna, Child of David   34
Make a Joyful Noise   30
My God, My God   41
O Day of Sad Remembrance   40
O God, We Come   33
Our God Created   36
This Solemn Night   39
We Praise You, Our Creator   28
We Who Stumble   32
Worship God in Truth   31

LIGHT

A Dark, Expectant, Waiting World   5
Children of God   10
Eternal Light, Whose Glorious
    Gleam   84

Topical Index of Hymns   205

God Is the Word   13
Great God of All Mystery   24
Hosanna, Child of David   34
Light Dispels the Shadows   6
O God, We Come   33
O Sovereign God   79
Transfiguration Hymn   26
We Praise You for Your Mercy   21
We Wait upon the Mountain   25
We Who Stumble   32

MERCY

All That Our God Has Spoken   68
Amid Our Fears   55
Come, All People, Sing   81
Defender of All   59
Give Ear to All God Teaches   66
God Reigns   72
Jesus the Christ, Who Came to
  Earth   12
My God, My God   41
O God, Our Souls Are Grateful   62

MINISTRY AND MISSION

Awaken, My People   1
Come, God's Own People   27
Give Ear to All God Teaches   66
God Is Our Refuge   56
God Wakens Us Today   35
Great God of All Mystery   24
O God, Who Names Us Servants   18
We Claim the Call   85

PEACE

Awaken, My People   1
Be with Us Here   74
Come, Meek of the Earth   2
Emmanuel Is Drawing Near   4
God Is the Word   13
God Takes Us by the Hand   17
O God, We Come   33
Sing the Praise of God   73
The Spirit Among Us   52
Trumpets and Voices   7

PENITENCE

Defender of All   59
Light Dispels the Shadows   6
O Rock and Redeemer   70
Our God, You Grant Us Rest   77
Our Shepherd and Our Rescuer   80
Sing the Praise of God   73

We Praise You for Your Mercy   21
We Praise You, Our Creator   28

PENTECOST SEASON

All That Our God Has Spoken   68
Amid Our Fears   55
At the Feet of Jesus   64
Be with Us, God   58
Be with Us Here   74
Come, All People, Sing   81
Come, Let Us Sing to God   67
Defender of All   59
Give Ear to All God Teaches   66
Give Thanks to God   63
Glory Be to Our Creator   69
God Is Our Refuge   56
God of Cloud and Burning Fire   65
God Reigns   72
In Awe, We Come to Worship   53
In Faithful Love Abiding   75
O God, Our Souls Are Grateful   62
O Love, Beyond All Knowing   76
O Rock and Redeemer   70
O Sovereign God   79
Our God, You Grant Us Rest   77
Our Shepherd and Our Rescuer   80
Sing the Praise of God   73
Spirit of God, Revive   51
Surely, Our God Is in This Place   57
The Heavens Declare Your Glory   78
The Spirit Among Us   52
Venture, All People   54
We Live Today   71

PRAYER

Amid Our Fears   55
Awaken, My People   1
Come, Believers, Sing Your Praises   11
Come, God's Own People   27
Defender of All   59
Give Thanks to God   63
Great God of All Mystery   24
Hear Now Our Prayer, O Lord   37
O God, to Whom   60
The Heavens Declare Your Glory   78
This Solemn Night   39

RESURRECTION

At the Feet of Jesus   64
Celebrate with Joy and Singing   43
Lord, Who Is It?   38
O God, We Come   33
O God, Who Names Us Servants   18

Topical Index of Hymns   207

Index of Scripture Readings

2:13–15, 19–23	First Sunday After Christmas
3:1–12	Second Sunday of Advent
3:13–17	First Sunday After Epiphany (Baptism of Our Sovereign)
4:1–11	First Sunday of Lent
4:12–23	Third Sunday After Epiphany
5:1–12	Fourth Sunday After Epiphany
5:13–16	Fifth Sunday After Epiphany
5:17–26	Sixth Sunday After Epiphany
5:27–37	Seventh Sunday After Epiphany
5:38–48	Eighth Sunday After Epiphany
6:1–6, 16–21	Ash Wednesday
7:15–29	Second Sunday After Pentecost
9:9–13	Third Sunday After Pentecost
9:35—10:15	Fourth Sunday After Pentecost
10:16–33	Fifth Sunday After Pentecost
10:34–42	Sixth Sunday After Pentecost
11:2–11	Third Sunday of Advent
11:25–30	Seventh Sunday After Pentecost
13:1–9, 18–23	Eighth Sunday After Pentecost
13:24–30, 36–43	Ninth Sunday After Pentecost
13:44–52	Tenth Sunday After Pentecost
14:13–21	Eleventh Sunday After Pentecost
14:22–33	Twelfth Sunday After Pentecost
15:21–28	Thirteenth Sunday After Pentecost
15:32–38	Eleventh Sunday After Pentecost (Parallel Passage)
16:13–20	Fourteenth Sunday After Pentecost
16:21–28	Fifteenth Sunday After Pentecost
17:1–9	Last Sunday After Epiphany (Transfiguration)
18:15–20	Sixteenth Sunday After Pentecost
18:21–35	Seventeenth Sunday After Pentecost
20:1–16	Eighteenth Sunday After Pentecost
21:1–11	Sixth Sunday of Lent (Palm Sunday)
21:28–32	Nineteenth Sunday After Pentecost
21:33–43	Twentieth Sunday After Pentecost
22:1–14	Twenty-first Sunday After Pentecost
22:15–22	Twenty-second Sunday After Pentecost
22:34–46	Twenty-third Sunday After Pentecost
23:1–12	Twenty-fourth Sunday After Pentecost
24:36–44	First Sunday of Advent
25:1–13	Twenty-fifth Sunday After Pentecost
25:14–30	Twenty-sixth Sunday After Pentecost
25:31–46	New Year's Day
	Last Sunday After Pentecost
26:14—27:66	Passion Sunday (Sixth Sunday of Lent)
27:11–54	Passion Sunday (Sixth Sunday of Lent)
28:1–10	Easter Sunday (Alternate Reading)
28:16–20	Trinity Sunday

MARK (These passages parallel the readings from Matthew; only the last one is in the Series A Lectionary.)

1:3–8	Second Sunday of Advent
1:9–11	First Sunday After Epiphany

1:12–13	First Sunday of Lent
2:13–17	Third Sunday After Pentecost
3:16–19	Fourth Sunday After Pentecost
4:1–20	Eighth Sunday After Pentecost
4:26–29	Ninth Sunday After Pentecost
6:8–11	Fourth Sunday After Pentecost
6:32–44	Eleventh Sunday After Pentecost
6:45–52	Twelfth Sunday After Pentecost
7:24–30	Thirteenth Sunday After Pentecost
8:27–30	Fourteenth Sunday After Pentecost
8:31—9:1	Fifteenth Sunday After Pentecost
11:1–10	Sixth Sunday of Lent (Palm Sunday)
12:1–12	Twentieth Sunday After Pentecost
12:13–17	Twenty-second Sunday After Pentecost
12:18–37	Twenty-third Sunday After Pentecost
12:38–39	Twenty-fifth Sunday After Pentecost
13:9–13	Fifth Sunday After Pentecost
14:10—15:47	Sixth Sunday of Lent (Passion Sunday)
16:1–8	Easter Sunday (Alternate Reading)
16:9–16, 19–20	Ascension Day

LUKE (Except for the first three, the last two, and Thanksgiving Day, these are not in the Series A Lectionary but are parallel to the Gospel readings from Matthew.)

2:1–20	Christmas Eve/Day
2:8–20	Christmas (Alternate Reading 1)
2:15–21	Celebration of Jesus and Mary (January 1)
3:2–17	Second Sunday of Advent
3:21–22	First Sunday After Epiphany
4:1–13	First Sunday of Lent
5:27–32	Third Sunday After Pentecost
6:14–16	Fourth Sunday After Pentecost
6:20–26	Fourth Sunday After Epiphany
6:27–36	Eighth Sunday After Epiphany
6:43–49	Second Sunday After Pentecost
7:18–30	Third Sunday of Advent
8:4–15	Eighth Sunday After Pentecost
9:3–5	Fourth Sunday After Pentecost
9:10–17	Eleventh Sunday After Pentecost
9:18–21	Fourteenth Sunday After Pentecost
9:22–27	Fifteenth Sunday After Pentecost
10:4–12	Fourth Sunday After Pentecost
10:21–22	Seventh Sunday After Pentecost
10:25–28	Twenty-third Sunday After Pentecost
11:39–52	Twenty-fourth Sunday After Pentecost
12:11–12	Fifth Sunday After Pentecost
14:16–24	Twenty-first Sunday After Pentecost
17:11–19	Thanksgiving Day
19:29–38	Sixth Sunday of Lent (Palm Sunday)
20:9–19	Twentieth Sunday After Pentecost
20:20–26, 41–44	Twenty-second Sunday After Pentecost
20:45–46	Twenty-fourth Sunday After Pentecost
21:12–19	Fifth Sunday After Pentecost

Index of Scripture Readings   215

PHILIPPIANS

1:1–11, 19–27	Eighteenth Sunday After Pentecost
2:1–13	Nineteenth Sunday After Pentecost
2:5–11	Sixth Sunday of Lent (Palm Sunday)
	Sixth Sunday of Lent (Passion Sunday)
2:9–13	Celebration of Jesus and Mary (January 1)
3:12–21	Twentieth Sunday After Pentecost
4:1–20	Twenty-first Sunday After Pentecost

COLOSSIANS

3:1–11	Easter Sunday

1 THESSALONIANS

1:1–10	Twenty-second Sunday After Pentecost
2:1–8	Twenty-third Sunday After Pentecost
2:9–13, 17–20	Twenty-fourth Sunday After Pentecost
4:13–18	Twenty-fifth Sunday After Pentecost
5:1–11	Twenty-sixth Sunday After Pentecost

TITUS

2:11–15	Christmas Eve/Day
3:4–7	Christmas Day (Alternate Reading 1)

HEBREWS

1:1–12	Christmas Day (Alternate Reading 2)
2:10–18	First Sunday After Christmas
4:14–16; 5:7–9	Good Friday
9:11–15	Monday of Holy Week
12:1–3	Wednesday of Holy Week

JAMES

5:7–10	Third Sunday of Advent

1 PETER

1:3–9	Second Sunday of Easter
1:17–23	Third Sunday of Easter
2:2–10	Fifth Sunday of Easter
2:19–25	Fourth Sunday of Easter
3:13–22	Sixth Sunday of Easter
4:12–14; 5:6–11	Seventh Sunday of Easter

2 PETER

1:16–21	Last Sunday After Epiphany (Transfiguration)

REVELATION

21:1–6a	New Year's Day

Index of Themes and Key Words

Abundance	January 1—Celebration of Jesus and Mary
	Second Sunday of Lent

	Monday of Holy Week Thanksgiving Day
Abundant life	Eighth Sunday After Epiphany Fourth Sunday of Easter Sixth Sunday After Pentecost Seventh Sunday After Pentecost Thirteenth Sunday After Pentecost
Acceptable time	Ash Wednesday
Acceptance	Third Sunday of Lent Second Sunday After Pentecost Third Sunday After Pentecost
Accountability	Second Sunday of Easter Sixteenth Sunday After Pentecost Seventeenth Sunday After Pentecost Twenty-sixth Sunday After Pentecost
Adoption	January 1—Celebration of Jesus and Mary Fifth Sunday of Lent Eighth Sunday After Pentecost
Alpha/Omega	January 1—New Year's Day
Amazement	January 1—Celebration of Jesus and Mary Second Sunday After Epiphany Tuesday of Holy Week Easter Sunday Pentecost Sunday
Anger	Fifth Sunday After Pentecost Sixteenth Sunday After Pentecost Twenty-third Sunday After Pentecost
Anticipation	First Sunday of Advent Second Sunday of Advent Last Sunday After Epiphany (Transfiguration) Third Sunday of Lent
Anxiety	Wednesday of Holy Week Seventh Sunday of Easter Fifth Sunday After Pentecost
Appearances	Second Sunday of Advent Ash Wednesday Fourth Sunday of Lent
Arrogance	Third Sunday of Lent Fourteenth Sunday After Pentecost Nineteenth Sunday After Pentecost
Ascension	Ascension

Ask	Tenth Sunday After Pentecost
Assurance	Fourth Sunday of Advent
	Christmas Day (Alternate 2)
	Second Sunday After Epiphany
	Sixth Sunday of Easter
	Seventh Sunday After Pentecost
	Tenth Sunday After Pentecost
Authenticity	Ash Wednesday
	Fourth Sunday of Lent
	Easter Sunday
Awaken	First Sunday of Advent
	Fourth Sunday of Lent
	Sixth Sunday of Lent (Passion Sunday)
	Sixth Sunday of Lent (Palm Sunday)
	Wednesday of Holy Week
Awe	Christmas Day (Alternate 1)
	Last Sunday After Epiphany (Transfiguration)
	Easter Sunday
	Ninth Sunday After Pentecost
	Fourteenth Sunday After Pentecost
	Eighteenth Sunday After Pentecost
	Twentieth Sunday After Pentecost
	Twenty-fourth Sunday After Pentecost
	Thanksgiving Day
Bad example	Twenty-fourth Sunday After Pentecost
Baptism	First Sunday After Epiphany (Baptism of Our Sovereign)
	Ascension
	Sixth Sunday After Pentecost
Bearing fruit	Second Sunday of Advent
	Second Sunday After Christmas
	Tuesday of Holy Week
	Second Sunday After Pentecost
	Twentieth Sunday After Pentecost
	Last Sunday After Pentecost
Beatitudes	Fourth Sunday After Epiphany
Believe	Second Sunday of Lent
	Sixth Sunday of Lent (Palm Sunday)
	Good Friday
	Second Sunday of Easter
	Third Sunday of Easter
	Third Sunday After Pentecost
	Fifth Sunday After Pentecost
Betrayal	Sixth Sunday of Lent (Passion Sunday)

	Sixth Sunday of Lent (Palm Sunday)
	Wednesday of Holy Week
Bewilderment	Last Sunday After Epiphany (Transfiguration)
	Pentecost Sunday
	Seventh Sunday After Pentecost
Birth	Christmas Eve/Day
	Christmas Day (Alternate 1)
Blessing	January 1—Celebration of Jesus and Mary
	Second Sunday After Christmas
	Second Sunday of Lent
	Second Sunday After Pentecost
	Fourth Sunday After Pentecost
	Ninth Sunday After Pentecost
	Eleventh Sunday After Pentecost
	Twenty-fourth Sunday After Pentecost
Blindness	Third Sunday of Advent
	Fourth Sunday of Lent
	Tenth Sunday After Pentecost
Blood	Third Sunday of Easter
	Pentecost Sunday
	Eleventh Sunday After Pentecost
Body of Christ	Second Sunday After Christmas
	Epiphany
	First Sunday of Lent
	Maundy Thursday
	Ascension
	Third Sunday After Pentecost
Bondage	Christmas Eve/Day
	First Sunday After Christmas
	Third Sunday After Epiphany
	Fifth Sunday of Lent
	Seventh Sunday After Pentecost
	Ninth Sunday After Pentecost
Born anew	Second Sunday of Lent
	Easter Sunday (Alternate)
	Second Sunday of Easter
	Third Sunday of Easter
Bounty	January 1—New Year's Day
	Twenty-first Sunday After Pentecost
	Thanksgiving Day
Bread	January 1—New Year's Day
	First Sunday of Lent
	Fourth Sunday of Easter
	Eleventh Sunday After Pentecost

Bread of Life	January 1-New Year's Day
	First Sunday of Lent
	Eleventh Sunday After Pentecost
Break bread	Maundy Thursday
	Third Sunday of Easter
Breath of Life	First Sunday After Epiphany (Baptism of Our Sovereign)
	Fifth Sunday of Lent
	Monday of Holy Week
Brother/sisterhood	First Sunday After Christmas
Build	Christmas Eve/Day
	Easter Sunday (Alternate)
	Second Sunday After Pentecost
	Sixteenth Sunday After Pentecost
	Seventeenth Sunday After Pentecost
Burden	Christmas Eve/Day
	Christmas Day (Alternate 2)
	Sixth Sunday of Lent (Passion Sunday)
	Maundy Thursday
	Seventh Sunday After Pentecost
	Eighth Sunday After Pentecost
	Twenty-fourth Sunday After Pentecost
	Twenty-sixth Sunday After Pentecost
Burning bush	Ninth Sunday After Pentecost
Caesarea Philippi	Fourteenth Sunday After Pentecost
Called/chosen	Twenty-first Sunday After Pentecost
Called by name	Second Sunday After Epiphany
	Tuesday of Holy Week
	Third Sunday of Easter
	Twenty-second Sunday After Pentecost
Caring	Fifth Sunday After Epiphany
	Seventh Sunday After Epiphany
	Eighth Sunday After Epiphany
	Last Sunday After Epiphany (Transfiguration)
	Twenty-fifth Sunday After Pentecost
Celebration	January 1—Celebration of Jesus and Mary
	Easter Sunday (Alternate)
	Ascension
	Thanksgiving Day
Ceremonies	Eleventh Sunday After Pentecost
Challenges	Second Sunday of Lent

	Maundy Thursday
	Pentecost Sunday
	Ninth Sunday After Pentecost
Change	Christmas Eve/Day
	Ash Wednesday
	Monday of Holy Week
	Pentecost Sunday
	Twenty-fifth Sunday After Pentecost
Child	Christmas Eve/Day
	Christmas Day (Alternate 1)
	Christmas Day (Alternate 2)
Children of God	Second Sunday After Christmas
	Fifth Sunday of Lent
	Sixth Sunday of Lent (Passion Sunday)
	Eighth Sunday After Pentecost
	Twenty-fourth Sunday After Pentecost
Children of night/day	Twenty-sixth Sunday After Pentecost
Choices	Sixth Sunday After Epiphany
	Seventh Sunday of Easter
	Sixth Sunday After Pentecost
Chosen	Second Sunday After Christmas
	Second Sunday After Epiphany
	Tuesday of Holy Week
	Fifth Sunday of Easter
	Twelfth Sunday After Pentecost
	Thirteenth Sunday After Pentecost
	Twenty-first Sunday After Pentecost
	Twenty-second Sunday After Pentecost
Christ: Cornerstone of faith	Fifth Sunday of Easter
Christ: Suffering Servant	Good Friday
Christ's coming	First Sunday of Advent
	Second Sunday of Advent
	January 1—Celebration of Jesus and Mary
	Twenty-fifth Sunday After Pentecost
Christ's commission	Ascension
	Trinity Sunday
Christ's example	Sixth Sunday of Lent (Passion Sunday)
	Tuesday of Holy Week
	Maundy Thursday
	Good Friday
	Second Sunday of Easter
	Eighteenth Sunday After Pentecost

| Christ's hands and feet | Wednesday of Holy Week |
| | Last Sunday After Pentecost |

Christ's lead	First Sunday of Advent
	Christmas Eve/Day
	First Sunday After Christmas
	Pentecost Sunday

Christ's presence	Last Sunday After Epiphany (Transfiguration)
	Sixth Sunday After Pentecost
	Eleventh Sunday After Pentecost

Church	Second Sunday of Easter
	Fourth Sunday of Easter
	Ascension
	Fourteenth Sunday After Pentecost
	Sixteenth Sunday After Pentecost

| Civil disobedience | Fifth Sunday of Easter |

| Cleverness | Tuesday of Holy Week |

| Cloud and fire | Ascension |
| | Tenth Sunday After Pentecost |

| Cloud of witnesses | Wednesday of Holy Week |

Comfort	Christmas Day (Alternate 2)
	Seventh Sunday After Epiphany
	Twenty-fifth Sunday After Pentecost

Commandments	Sixth Sunday After Epiphany
	Second Sunday After Pentecost
	Thirteenth Sunday After Pentecost
	Sixteenth Sunday After Pentecost
	Twenty-third Sunday After Pentecost

Commitment	Epiphany
	Ash Wednesday
	Fourth Sunday of Lent
	Second Sunday After Pentecost
	Twelfth Sunday After Pentecost
	Sixteenth Sunday After Pentecost
	Nineteenth Sunday After Pentecost
	Twenty-fourth Sunday After Pentecost

| Commonplace | Fourth Sunday After Epiphany |

| Commonwealth of heaven | Twentieth Sunday After Pentecost |

Community of faith	Easter Sunday (Alternate)
	Third Sunday of Easter
	Second Sunday After Pentecost
	Fifteenth Sunday After Pentecost

Company of saints	Second Sunday After Epiphany
	Ascension
Compassion	Sixth Sunday After Epiphany
	Seventh Sunday After Epiphany
	Tuesday of Holy Week
	Fourth Sunday After Pentecost
	Eleventh Sunday After Pentecost
	Fifteenth Sunday After Pentecost
	Sixteenth Sunday After Pentecost
	Twenty-third Sunday After Pentecost
Complaints	Last Sunday After Epiphany (Transfiguration)
	Second Sunday of Lent
	Third Sunday of Lent
	Fourth Sunday After Pentecost
Confidence	Epiphany
	Third Sunday of Easter
	Tenth Sunday After Pentecost
	Nineteenth Sunday After Pentecost
	Twenty-second Sunday After Pentecost
Courage	Monday of Holy Week
	Third Sunday of Easter
	Ninth Sunday After Pentecost
Covenant	First Sunday After Christmas
	First Sunday After Epiphany (Baptism of Our Sovereign)
	Seventh Sunday After Epiphany
	Monday of Holy Week
	Fourth Sunday of Easter
	Fourth Sunday After Pentecost
	Tenth Sunday After Pentecost
	Thirteenth Sunday After Pentecost
	Fifteenth Sunday After Pentecost
	Twenty-fourth Sunday After Pentecost
Creation	Trinity Sunday
	Ninth Sunday After Pentecost
	Fourteenth Sunday After Pentecost
Creeds	Thirteenth Sunday After Pentecost
Cross	Fourth Sunday After Epiphany
	Sixth Sunday of Lent (Passion Sunday)
	Sixth Sunday of Lent (Palm Sunday)
	Tuesday of Holy Week
	Wednesday of Holy Week
	Sixth Sunday After Pentecost
Crown of thorns	Sixth Sunday of Lent (Palm Sunday)

Index of Themes and Key Words   223

Different drummer	Twelfth Sunday After Pentecost
Discipleship	Epiphany
	First Sunday After Epiphany (Baptism of Our Sovereign)
	Third Sunday After Epiphany
	Sixth Sunday of Lent (Passion Sunday)
	Easter Sunday (Alternate)
	Fourth Sunday of Easter
	Ascension
	Seventh Sunday of Easter
	Pentecost Sunday
	Trinity Sunday
	Fourth Sunday After Pentecost
	Fifth Sunday After Pentecost
Distorting reality	Fourteenth Sunday After Pentecost
Dominion	Ascension
	Trinity Sunday
Doubt	Third Sunday of Advent
	Fourth Sunday of Advent
	Fourth Sunday After Epiphany
	Ascension
	Eighth Sunday After Pentecost
	Twelfth Sunday After Pentecost
Dreams	Pentecost Sunday
Dry bones	Fifth Sunday of Lent
Ears	Third Sunday of Advent
	Sixth Sunday of Lent (Passion Sunday)
	Sixth Sunday of Lent (Palm Sunday)
	Third Sunday of Easter
Elisha	Sixth Sunday After Pentecost
Eloquence	Second Sunday After Epiphany
Emmanuel	Fourth Sunday of Advent
Emmaus road	Third Sunday After Pentecost
Empowerment	Second Sunday After Christmas
	Seventh Sunday After Epiphany
	Ash Wednesday
	Fifth Sunday of Lent
	Seventh Sunday of Easter
	Trinity Sunday
	Sixteenth Sunday After Pentecost
	Twentieth Sunday After Pentecost

226   Index of Themes and Key Words

Index of Themes and Key Words   227

	Third Sunday of Lent
	Easter Sunday (Alternate)
	Sixth Sunday of Easter
	Sixteenth Sunday After Pentecost
Faithlessness	Twenty-fourth Sunday After Pentecost
Fear	Third Sunday of Advent
	Fourth Sunday of Advent
	Second Sunday of Lent
	Monday of Holy Week
	Tuesday of Holy Week
	Wednesday of Holy Week
	Maundy Thursday
	Easter Sunday
	Fourth Sunday of Easter
	Seventh Sunday of Easter
	Fifth Sunday After Pentecost
	Twelfth Sunday After Pentecost
	Fourteenth Sunday After Pentecost
	Twenty-second Sunday After Pentecost
	Twenty-sixth Sunday After Pentecost
Feast	Monday of Holy Week
Fine pearls	Tenth Sunday After Pentecost
Fire	Last Sunday After Epiphany (Transfiguration)
	Pentecost Sunday
First/last	Pentecost Sunday
	Second Sunday After Pentecost
Flesh	Christmas Day (Alternate 2)
	Sixth Sunday of Lent (Passion Sunday)
	Seventh Sunday After Pentecost
	Eighth Sunday After Pentecost
Follow	Epiphany
	Second Sunday of Lent
	Tuesday of Holy Week
	Wednesday of Holy Week
	Fifth Sunday of Easter
	Sixth Sunday of Easter
	Seventh Sunday of Easter
	Fourteenth Sunday After Pentecost
	Twenty-second Sunday After Pentecost
	Last Sunday After Pentecost
Follow me	Third Sunday After Epiphany
	Third Sunday After Pentecost
Foolishness	Fourth Sunday After Epiphany

	Tuesday of Holy Week
	Second Sunday After Pentecost
Fools for Christ	Seventh Sunday After Epiphany
Foot washing	Maundy Thursday
Forgiveness	Second Sunday of Lent
	Third Sunday of Lent
	Maundy Thursday
	Good Friday
	Easter Sunday
	Easter Sunday (Alternate)
	Second Sunday of Easter
	Ascension
	Pentecost Sunday
	Third Sunday After Pentecost
	Fourth Sunday After Pentecost
	Ninth Sunday After Pentecost
	Sixteenth Sunday After Pentecost
	Seventeenth Sunday After Pentecost
Forsaken	Sixth Sunday of Lent (Passion Sunday)
Freedom	First Sunday After Christmas
	Third Sunday After Epiphany
	Fifth Sunday of Lent
	Seventh Sunday After Pentecost
	Eighth Sunday After Pentecost
	Ninth Sunday After Pentecost
Fruit	Third Sunday of Advent
	Easter Sunday (Alternate)
	Second Sunday After Pentecost
	Twentieth Sunday After Pentecost
Fruitful labor	Eighteenth Sunday After Pentecost
Fruits of the Spirit	Second Sunday After Pentecost
	Ninth Sunday After Pentecost
Fulfillment	Ascension
	Seventh Sunday After Pentecost
Generosity	January 1—Celebration of Jesus and Mary
	Seventh Sunday After Epiphany
	Third Sunday of Easter
	Fourth Sunday of Easter
	Eighteenth Sunday After Pentecost
	Twenty-sixth Sunday After Pentecost
	Last Sunday After Pentecost
	Thanksgiving Day

Gentleness	Sixth Sunday of Easter
	Third Sunday After Pentecost
	Seventh Sunday After Pentecost
Genuineness	Ash Wednesday
	Second Sunday of Easter
	Sixteenth Sunday After Pentecost
Giving	Third Sunday of Easter
	Sixth Sunday After Pentecost
	Sixteenth Sunday After Pentecost
	Thanksgiving Day
Giving your best	Twenty-fourth Sunday After Pentecost
Gladness	Third Sunday of Advent
	Easter Sunday
	Easter Sunday (Alternate)
	Second Sunday of Easter
	Third Sunday of Easter
Gloom	Third Sunday After Epiphany
	Twenty-second Sunday After Pentecost
	Twenty-fifth Sunday After Pentecost
	Twenty-sixth Sunday After Pentecost
God's anger	Twenty-fourth Sunday After Pentecost
	Twenty-sixth Sunday After Pentecost
God's call	Second Sunday After Epiphany
	Tuesday of Holy Week
	Third Sunday of Easter
	Fifth Sunday of Easter
	Thirteenth Sunday After Pentecost
	Nineteenth Sunday After Pentecost
	Twentieth Sunday After Pentecost
	Twenty-first Sunday After Pentecost
	Twenty-second Sunday After Pentecost
God's care	January 1—New Year's Day
	Seventh Sunday After Epiphany
	Third Sunday of Lent
	Fifth Sunday of Easter
	Seventh Sunday of Easter
	Trinity Sunday
	Tenth Sunday After Pentecost
	Twentieth Sunday After Pentecost
	Twenty-first Sunday After Pentecost
	Last Sunday After Pentecost
	Thanksgiving Day
God's counsel	Second Sunday of Easter

God's family	Ninth Sunday After Pentecost Thirteenth Sunday After Pentecost
God's favor	Twenty-third Sunday After Pentecost Twenty-fourth Sunday After Pentecost
God's gift(s)	Fourth Sunday of Advent Christmas Eve/Day Christmas Day (Alternate 1) Ash Wednesday First Sunday of Lent Second Sunday of Lent Sixth Sunday of Lent (Passion Sunday) Second Sunday of Easter Fourth Sunday of Easter Ninth Sunday After Pentecost Tenth Sunday After Pentecost Thirteenth Sunday After Pentecost Fifteenth Sunday After Pentecost Seventeenth Sunday After Pentecost Twentieth Sunday After Pentecost Twenty-first Sunday After Pentecost Thanksgiving Day
God's glory	Christmas Day (Alternate 1) January 1—Celebration of Jesus and Mary Epiphany Last Sunday After Epiphany (Transfiguration) Monday of Holy Week
God's goodness	Christmas Day (Alternate 1) January 1—New Year's Day Tuesday of Holy Week Trinity Sunday Seventeenth Sunday After Pentecost Thanksgiving Day
God's greatness	Tuesday of Holy Week Fourteenth Sunday After Pentecost Twenty-first Sunday After Pentecost
God's invitation	Twenty-first Sunday After Pentecost
God's kindness	Christmas Day (Alternate 1) First Sunday After Christmas Fifth Sunday of Easter Twenty-first Sunday After Pentecost
God's law	First Sunday of Advent Third Sunday After Epiphany Fifth Sunday After Epiphany Sixth Sunday After Epiphany Eighth Sunday After Epiphany

God's lead	Fourth Sunday of Easter
	Fifteenth Sunday After Pentecost
	Twenty-second Sunday After Pentecost
God's love	First Sunday of Advent
	Fourth Sunday of Advent
	Eighth Sunday After Epiphany
	Last Sunday After Epiphany (Transfiguration)
	Ash Wednesday
	Second Sunday of Lent
	Fourth Sunday of Lent
	Sixth Sunday of Lent (Passion Sunday)
	Monday of Holy Week
	Maundy Thursday
	Good Friday
	Easter Sunday (Alternate)
	Sixth Sunday of Easter
	Seventh Sunday of Easter
	Twenty-third Sunday After Pentecost
God's power	Third Sunday After Epiphany
	Twelfth Sunday After Pentecost
God's presence	Fourth Sunday of Advent
	Christmas Day (Alternate 1)
	Christmas Day (Alternate 2)
	January 1—New Year's Day
	First Sunday After Christmas
	Fifth Sunday After Epiphany
	Last Sunday After Epiphany (Transfiguration)
	Fourth Sunday of Lent
	Fifth Sunday After Pentecost
	Eleventh Sunday After Pentecost
	Fifteenth Sunday After Pentecost
	Twenty-third Sunday After Pentecost
	Twenty-fifth Sunday After Pentecost
	Last Sunday After Pentecost
God's promise(s)	Second Sunday of Advent
	Third Sunday of Advent
	Christmas Eve/Day
	Second Sunday After Epiphany
	Second Sunday of Lent
	Easter Sunday (Alternate)
	Third Sunday of Easter
	Seventh Sunday of Easter
	Pentecost Sunday
	Third Sunday After Pentecost
	Ninth Sunday After Pentecost
God's purposes	Second Sunday of Advent
	Fourth Sunday of Advent
	Christmas Eve/Day

	Sixth Sunday After Pentecost Fourteenth Sunday After Pentecost Nineteenth Sunday After Pentecost
God's realm	Ascension Fourth Sunday After Pentecost Eighth Sunday After Pentecost Twentieth Sunday After Pentecost
God's reign	Christmas Day (Alternate 2) Second Sunday After Christmas Twenty-first Sunday After Pentecost Last Sunday After Pentecost
God's saving acts	January 1—Celebration of Jesus and Mary Fourth Sunday After Epiphany Twenty-sixth Sunday After Pentecost
God's surprises	Third Sunday of Advent Christmas Day (Alternate 1) Fourth Sunday of Lent Easter Sunday Pentecost Sunday Sixth Sunday After Pentecost
God's visitation	Second Sunday of Advent Christmas Day (Alternate 1) Christmas Day (Alternate 2) Second Sunday After Christmas Ascension Seventh Sunday of Easter
God's way(s)	First Sunday of Advent Sixth Sunday After Epiphany Second Sunday After Pentecost Twenty-second Sunday After Pentecost
God's work	January 1—Celebration of Jesus and Mary January 1—New Year's Day Sixth Sunday After Pentecost Eighteenth Sunday After Pentecost Nineteenth Sunday After Pentecost
Good/evil	Sixth Sunday After Epiphany Good Friday Seventh Sunday After Pentecost Tenth Sunday After Pentecost Seventeenth Sunday After Pentecost
Good earth	Thanksgiving Day
Good news	Third Sunday of Advent Christmas Eve/Day

Christmas Day (Alternate 1)
Christmas Day (Alternate 2)
January 1—Celebration of Jesus and Mary
Epiphany
Easter Sunday
Easter Sunday (Alternate)
Seventh Sunday After Pentecost
Eighteenth Sunday After Pentecost
Twenty-third Sunday After Pentecost

Good Shepherd

Fourth Sunday of Easter
Last Sunday After Pentecost

Goodness

Easter Sunday
Third Sunday After Pentecost

Grace

First Sunday of Advent
Fourth Sunday of Advent
Christmas Day (Alternate 1)
Christmas Day (Alternate 2)
January 1—Celebration of Jesus and Mary
Second Sunday After Epiphany
Ash Wednesday
First Sunday of Lent
Monday of Holy Week
Second Sunday After Pentecost
Third Sunday After Pentecost
Fifth Sunday After Pentecost
Sixth Sunday After Pentecost
Eleventh Sunday After Pentecost

Gratitude

January 1—New Year's Day
Second Sunday After Christmas
Seventeenth Sunday After Pentecost
Eighteenth Sunday After Pentecost
Twenty-first Sunday After Pentecost
Thanksgiving Day

Graven images

First Sunday After Epiphany (Baptism of Our
    Sovereign)
Monday of Holy Week

Grief

Good Friday
Twenty-fifth Sunday After Pentecost

Guilt

Sixth Sunday of Lent (Passion Sunday)
Eighth Sunday After Pentecost
Eighteenth Sunday After Pentecost

Hand

Christmas Day (Alternate 2)
Second Sunday After Christmas
First Sunday After Epiphany (Baptism of Our
    Sovereign)

Sixth Sunday After Epiphany
Seventh Sunday After Epiphany
Ash Wednesday
Sixth Sunday of Lent (Passion Sunday)
Monday of Holy Week
Tuesday of Holy Week
Maundy Thursday
Second Sunday of Easter
Fifth Sunday of Easter
Seventh Sunday of Easter
Trinity Sunday
Eleventh Sunday After Pentecost
Fourteenth Sunday After Pentecost
Eighteenth Sunday After Pentecost
Twentieth Sunday After Pentecost
Twenty-first Sunday After Pentecost
Twenty-second Sunday After Pentecost

Harmony

Second Sunday of Advent
Ninth Sunday After Pentecost
Fifteenth Sunday After Pentecost

Harvest

Third Sunday of Advent
Third Sunday of Lent
Fourth Sunday After Pentecost
Twentieth Sunday After Pentecost
Thanksgiving Day

Hasten

Wednesday of Holy Week

Healing

January 1—Celebration of Jesus and Mary
First Sunday After Epiphany (Baptism of Our
   Sovereign)
Eighth Sunday After Epiphany
Ash Wednesday
Fourth Sunday of Lent
Sixth Sunday of Lent (Palm Sunday)
Good Friday
Easter Sunday
Easter Sunday (Alternate)
Third Sunday After Pentecost
Fourth Sunday After Pentecost
Ninth Sunday After Pentecost
Eleventh Sunday After Pentecost
Fifteenth Sunday After Pentecost

Heart, soul, mind

Twenty-third Sunday After Pentecost

Hearts

Epiphany
Sixth Sunday After Epiphany
Sixth Sunday of Lent (Palm Sunday)
Maundy Thursday
Good Friday

Fifth Sunday After Epiphany
Sixth Sunday of Lent (Palm Sunday)
Maundy Thursday
Seventh Sunday of Easter
Seventh Sunday After Pentecost
Twenty-fourth Sunday After Pentecost

Hunger
January 1—New Year's Day
Fifth Sunday After Epiphany
Seventh Sunday After Epiphany
Eighth Sunday After Epiphany
Sixth Sunday of Easter

Idols
Fourth Sunday of Lent
Fifth Sunday of Easter
Sixth Sunday of Easter
Sixteenth Sunday After Pentecost
Twenty-third Sunday After Pentecost

Inclusiveness
Second Sunday of Advent
Fifth Sunday of Easter
Thirteenth Sunday After Pentecost

Inheritance
Second Sunday After Christmas
Sixth Sunday After Epiphany
Monday of Holy Week
Ascension
Thanksgiving Day

Inner fire
Pentecost Sunday
Fifth Sunday After Pentecost

Insensitivity
Ninth Sunday After Pentecost

Intercession
Good Friday
Seventh Sunday of Easter
Eleventh Sunday After Pentecost
Twelfth Sunday After Pentecost

Isolation
Ninth Sunday After Pentecost
Tenth Sunday After Pentecost
Twenty-second Sunday After Pentecost

Jealousy
Eighteenth Sunday After Pentecost
Twenty-third Sunday After Pentecost

Jesus: Pioneer and Perfecter
Wednesday of Holy Week

Joy
Third Sunday of Advent
Christmas Eve/Day
Christmas Day (Alternate 2)
Third Sunday After Epiphany
Seventh Sunday After Epiphany

Light	First Sunday of Advent
	Christmas Eve/Day
	Christmas Day (Alternate 2)
	Epiphany
	Second Sunday After Epiphany
	Third Sunday After Epiphany
	Fifth Sunday After Epiphany
	Last Sunday After Epiphany (Transfiguration)
	Fourth Sunday of Lent
	Monday of Holy Week
	Trinity Sunday
	Twenty-second Sunday After Pentecost
	Twenty-fifth Sunday After Pentecost
	Twenty-sixth Sunday After Pentecost
	Last Sunday After Pentecost
Listen	Epiphany
	Third Sunday After Epiphany
	Eighth Sunday After Epiphany
	Third Sunday of Easter
	Fourth Sunday After Pentecost
Living Hope	Second Sunday of Easter
Living Water	Third Sunday of Advent
	January 1—New Year's Day
	Seventh Sunday After Epiphany
	Third Sunday of Lent
	Monday of Holy Week
	Fourteenth Sunday After Pentecost
Loaves/fish	Eleventh Sunday After Pentecost
Loneliness	Fourth Sunday of Advent
	Eleventh Sunday After Pentecost
	Twelfth Sunday After Pentecost
Longing	Seventh Sunday After Epiphany
	Last Sunday After Epiphany (Transfiguration)
	Ash Wednesday
	Eighth Sunday After Pentecost
	Twelfth Sunday After Pentecost
Love	Christmas Day (Alternate 1)
	First Sunday After Christmas
	Fifth Sunday After Epiphany
	Easter Sunday
	Third Sunday of Easter
	Ascension
	Trinity Sunday
	Second Sunday After Pentecost
	Third Sunday After Pentecost
	Eighteenth Sunday After Pentecost

Love of enemies	Eighth Sunday After Pentecost
	Sixteenth Sunday After Pentecost
Love of God	Twenty-third Sunday After Pentecost
Love of neighbor	First Sunday of Advent
	Eighth Sunday After Epiphany
	Sixteenth Sunday After Pentecost
	Twenty-third Sunday After Pentecost
Love of others	Maundy Thursday
	Third Sunday of Easter
	Sixth Sunday of Easter
Lowly	Fourth Sunday After Epiphany
	Eighth Sunday After Epiphany
	Last Sunday After Epiphany (Transfiguration)
	Seventh Sunday After Pentecost
Manger	Christmas Day (Alternate 1)
	January 1—Celebration of Jesus and Mary
	Fourth Sunday After Epiphany
Manna	January 1—New Year's Day
	Thirteenth Sunday After Pentecost
Manner of life	Eighteenth Sunday After Pentecost
Marriage feast	Twenty-first Sunday After Pentecost
Materialism	Ash Wednesday
	First Sunday of Lent
	Thanksgiving Day
Memorials	Eleventh Sunday After Pentecost
Memory	Third Sunday of Lent
Mercy	First Sunday After Christmas
	Fifth Sunday of Easter
	Seventh Sunday of Easter
	Second Sunday After Pentecost
	Ninth Sunday After Pentecost
	Thirteenth Sunday After Pentecost
	Seventeenth Sunday After Pentecost
	Thanksgiving Day
Merrymakers	Easter Sunday (Alternate)
Ministry	First Sunday After Epiphany (Baptism of Our Sovereign)
	Second Sunday After Epiphany
	Second Sunday of Lent

	Fourth Sunday of Easter
	Third Sunday After Pentecost
	Thirteenth Sunday After Pentecost
	Last Sunday After Pentecost
Miracles	January 1—Celebration of Jesus and Mary
	Eleventh Sunday After Pentecost
Mountain	First Sunday of Advent
	Second Sunday of Advent
	Christmas Day (Alternate 2)
	Seventh Sunday After Epiphany
	Last Sunday After Epiphany (Transfiguration)
	Tenth Sunday After Pentecost
	Fourteenth Sunday After Pentecost
	Twenty-first Sunday After Pentecost
	Twenty-second Sunday After Pentecost
	Thanksgiving Day
Mountaintops	Last Sunday After Epiphany (Transfiguration)
	Monday of Holy Week
	Ascension
	Ninth Sunday After Pentecost
Mystery of God	January 1—Celebration of Jesus and Mary
	Fifth Sunday After Epiphany
	Sixth Sunday After Epiphany
	First Sunday of Lent
	Sixth Sunday of Easter
	Fourteenth Sunday After Pentecost
Needy	January 1—New Year's Day
	Fifth Sunday After Epiphany
	Eighth Sunday After Epiphany
	Fourth Sunday After Pentecost
	Last Sunday After Pentecost
Neighbors	First Sunday of Advent
	Eighth Sunday After Epiphany
	Sixteenth Sunday After Pentecost
New commandment	Maundy Thursday
New heart	Nineteenth Sunday After Pentecost
New life	Second Sunday of Lent
	Third Sunday of Lent
	Fifth Sunday of Lent
	Easter Sunday
	Sixth Sunday After Pentecost
	Last Sunday After Pentecost
New nature	Easter Sunday

	Eighth Sunday After Epiphany Good Friday
Ordinary people	Sixth Sunday of Lent (Passion Sunday) Fourth Sunday After Pentecost
Other cheek	Eighth Sunday After Epiphany Sixth Sunday of Lent (Passion Sunday) Tuesday of Holy Week
Pain	Sixth Sunday of Lent (Passion Sunday) Good Friday Seventh Sunday of Easter Fourth Sunday After Pentecost Fifteenth Sunday After Pentecost
Partiality	Fourth Sunday of Advent January 1—Celebration of Jesus and Mary First Sunday After Epiphany (Baptism of Our Sovereign) Easter Sunday Twenty-fourth Sunday After Pentecost
Partnership	Eighteenth Sunday After Pentecost Twenty-first Sunday After Pentecost
Passover	Maundy Thursday
Patience	Third Sunday of Advent Third Sunday After Pentecost Seventeenth Sunday After Pentecost Twenty-fifth Sunday After Pentecost
Peace	First Sunday of Advent Second Sunday of Advent Christmas Eve/Day Christmas Day (Alternate 1) Christmas Day (Alternate 2) First Sunday After Epiphany (Baptism of Our Sovereign) Easter Sunday Second Sunday of Easter Sixth Sunday of Easter Trinity Sunday Third Sunday After Pentecost Fourth Sunday After Pentecost Seventh Sunday After Pentecost
Pity	Ninth Sunday After Pentecost
Playing God	First Sunday of Lent Fourth Sunday of Lent Nineteenth Sunday After Pentecost Twenty-second Sunday After Pentecost

Poor	Eighth Sunday After Epiphany
	Twenty-third Sunday After Pentecost
Positive/negative forces	Twelfth Sunday After Pentecost
Power	Second Sunday of Advent
	Last Sunday After Epiphany (Transfiguration)
	First Sunday of Lent
	Tuesday of Holy Week
	Easter Sunday
	Ascension
	Thanksgiving Day
Power of love	Tuesday of Holy Week
Practice what preach	Twenty-fourth Sunday After Pentecost
Praise	January 1—Celebration of Jesus and Mary
	January 1—New Year's Day
	Ascension
Prayer	Second Sunday After Christmas
	Seventh Sunday After Epiphany
	Eighth Sunday After Epiphany
	Fourth Sunday of Easter
	Seventh Sunday of Easter
	Sixteenth Sunday After Pentecost
	Twenty-first Sunday After Pentecost
	Thanksgiving Day
Preparation	First Sunday of Advent
	Fifth Sunday After Epiphany
	Sixth Sunday of Easter
	Twenty-fifth Sunday After Pentecost
Pride	Fourth Sunday After Epiphany
	First Sunday of Lent
	Thanksgiving Day
Prince of Peace	Christmas Eve/Day
Priorities	Christmas Eve/Day
	Third Sunday After Epiphany
	Sixth Sunday After Pentecost
Procrastination	Ash Wednesday
Prophecy	Last Sunday After Epiphany (Transfiguration)
	Fifteenth Sunday After Pentecost
Prophet(s)	Epiphany
	Fifth Sunday After Epiphany

	Sixth Sunday of Lent (Palm Sunday)
	Fourteenth Sunday After Pentecost
Reassurance	Twelfth Sunday After Pentecost
	Seventeenth Sunday After Pentecost
	Twenty-second Sunday After Pentecost
	Twenty-fifth Sunday After Pentecost
Rebellion	Sixteenth Sunday After Pentecost
	Twenty-second Sunday After Pentecost
Reconciliation	Sixth Sunday After Epiphany
	Ash Wednesday
	Third Sunday of Lent
	Maundy Thursday
	Fourth Sunday After Pentecost
	Sixth Sunday After Pentecost
	Thirteenth Sunday After Pentecost
	Sixteenth Sunday After Pentecost
Redemption	Fourth Sunday After Epiphany
	Ninth Sunday After Pentecost
	Eleventh Sunday After Pentecost
Refuge	Seventh Sunday After Epiphany
	Tuesday of Holy Week
	Fourth Sunday After Pentecost
	Twenty-first Sunday After Pentecost
Rejection	Good Friday
Rejoicing	Christmas Day (Alternate 1)
	Easter Sunday
	Twenty-first Sunday After Pentecost
Remembrance	Second Sunday After Christmas
	Good Friday
	Fourth Sunday of Easter
	Thanksgiving Day
Renewal	Third Sunday of Advent
	January 1—New Year's Day
	Second Sunday After Christmas
	Third Sunday After Epiphany
	Ash Wednesday
	Maundy Thursday
	Easter Sunday (Alternate)
	Trinity Sunday
	Third Sunday After Pentecost
	Fifteenth Sunday After Pentecost
Repentance	Second Sunday of Advent
	Ash Wednesday

	Maundy Thursday
	Nineteenth Sunday After Pentecost
	Twentieth Sunday After Pentecost
	Twenty-sixth Sunday After Pentecost
Rescue	Tuesday of Holy Week
	Last Sunday After Pentecost
Resentment	Fifth Sunday After Pentecost
	Sixteenth Sunday After Pentecost
	Eighteenth Sunday After Pentecost
Resistance	Fourth Sunday of Easter
	Pentecost Sunday
	Sixteenth Sunday After Pentecost
Responsibility	Second Sunday After Epiphany
	Tenth Sunday After Pentecost
	Twelfth Sunday After Pentecost
	Fourteenth Sunday After Pentecost
Responsiveness	Epiphany
	Third Sunday of Easter
	Pentecost Sunday
	Trinity Sunday
	Last Sunday After Pentecost
Rest	Seventh Sunday After Pentecost
Restoration	Fourth Sunday of Advent
	Seventh Sunday of Easter
	Fifteenth Sunday After Pentecost
	Twenty-fourth Sunday After Pentecost
Resurrection	Fifth Sunday of Lent
	Easter Sunday
	Easter Sunday (Alternate)
	Second Sunday of Easter
	Third Sunday After Pentecost
	Sixth Sunday After Pentecost
	Eighth Sunday After Pentecost
	Last Sunday After Pentecost
Revelation	Christmas Day (Alternate 2)
	Epiphany
Reverence	Sixth Sunday of Easter
Reward	Sixth Sunday After Pentecost
Righteousness	Christmas Eve/Day
	First Sunday After Epiphany (Baptism of Our

Sovereign)
Fourth Sunday After Epiphany
Fifth Sunday After Epiphany
First Sunday of Lent
Tuesday of Holy Week
Fourth Sunday of Easter
Sixth Sunday of Easter
Third Sunday After Pentecost
Twenty-fifth Sunday After Pentecost

Risen
Easter Sunday
Easter Sunday (Alternate)

Risk
Second Sunday of Lent
Third Sunday of Easter
Sixth Sunday After Pentecost

Rock
Seventh Sunday After Epiphany
Tuesday of Holy Week
Fifth Sunday of Easter
Second Sunday After Pentecost
Fourteenth Sunday After Pentecost

Sacrifice
Second Sunday of Lent
Third Sunday of Easter
Sixth Sunday of Easter
Fifteenth Sunday After Pentecost
Twenty-fourth Sunday After Pentecost
Last Sunday After Pentecost

Saints
Fourth Sunday of Advent
Second Sunday After Epiphany
Sixth Sunday After Pentecost

Salt
Fifth Sunday After Epiphany

Salvation
First Sunday of Advent
Third Sunday of Advent
Christmas Day (Alternate 1)
Christmas Day (Alternate 2)
January 1—Celebration of Jesus and Mary
Fourth Sunday After Epiphany
Ash Wednesday
Third Sunday of Lent
Tuesday of Holy Week
Good Friday
Easter Sunday
Easter Sunday (Alternate)
Pentecost Sunday
Fourth Sunday After Pentecost
Fifth Sunday After Pentecost
Eleventh Sunday After Pentecost

Last Sunday After Epiphany (Transfiguration)
Ash Wednesday
First Sunday of Lent
Second Sunday of Lent
Fifth Sunday of Lent
Sixth Sunday of Lent (Palm Sunday)
Monday of Holy Week
Maundy Thursday
Fourth Sunday of Easter
Fourth Sunday After Pentecost
Fifteenth Sunday After Pentecost
Eighteenth Sunday After Pentecost
Nineteenth Sunday After Pentecost
Twenty-fourth Sunday After Pentecost
Twenty-sixth Sunday After Pentecost

Shadow(s)

Christmas Eve/Day
Epiphany
Third Sunday After Epiphany
Twenty-fifth Sunday After Pentecost
Twenty-sixth Sunday After Pentecost
Last Sunday After Pentecost

Shame

Wednesday of Holy Week
Fifth Sunday of Easter

Shared humanity

Christmas Day (Alternate 2)
First Sunday After Christmas
January 1—Celebration of Jesus and Mary
Sixth Sunday of Lent (Passion Sunday)
Sixth Sunday of Lent (Palm Sunday)
Good Friday
Ascension

Sharing

Fourth Sunday of Advent
January 1—New Year's Day
Fifth Sunday After Epiphany
Sixth Sunday After Epiphany
Seventh Sunday After Epiphany
Second Sunday of Easter
Eleventh Sunday After Pentecost
Eighteenth Sunday After Pentecost

Sharing ourselves

Third Sunday After Epiphany
Fifth Sunday After Epiphany
Sixth Sunday After Pentecost
Twelfth Sunday After Pentecost
Nineteenth Sunday After Pentecost
Twenty-third Sunday After Pentecost
Twenty-fourth Sunday After Pentecost
Last Sunday After Pentecost

Sheep

Good Friday
Fifth Sunday After Pentecost

Solemn assemblies	Twenty-fifth Sunday After Pentecost
Sorrow	Good Friday Twelfth Sunday After Pentecost Twenty-fifth Sunday After Pentecost
Soul	Second Sunday of Easter Third Sunday of Easter Fourth Sunday of Easter Sixth Sunday of Easter Second Sunday After Pentecost Fifth Sunday After Pentecost Ninth Sunday After Pentecost Eleventh Sunday After Pentecost
Sower	Eighth Sunday After Pentecost
Spirit	First Sunday After Epiphany (Baptism of Our Sovereign) Sixth Sunday After Epiphany Fifth Sunday of Lent Trinity Sunday Second Sunday After Pentecost Seventh Sunday After Pentecost Eighth Sunday After Pentecost Nineteenth Sunday After Pentecost
Spiritual ancestors	First Sunday of Advent First Sunday of Lent Third Sunday of Lent Maundy Thursday Fourth Sunday of Easter Tenth Sunday After Pentecost Thanksgiving Day
Spiritual depths	Second Sunday After Christmas Third Sunday of Lent Eighth Sunday After Pentecost
Spiritual household	Fifth Sunday of Easter Last Sunday After Pentecost
Spiritual nourishment	Sixth Sunday After Epiphany First Sunday of Lent Third Sunday of Lent Fourth Sunday of Easter Fifth Sunday of Easter Sixth Sunday of Easter Seventh Sunday After Pentecost
Star	Epiphany Last Sunday After Epiphany (Transfiguration)

Status quo	Third Sunday of Easter
	Tenth Sunday After Pentecost
Steadfast love	First Sunday After Christmas
	January 1—New Year's Day
	Monday of Holy Week
	Fifth Sunday of Easter
	Second Sunday After Pentecost
	Third Sunday After Pentecost
	Ninth Sunday After Pentecost
	Tenth Sunday After Pentecost
	Eleventh Sunday After Pentecost
	Twelfth Sunday After Pentecost
	Sixteenth Sunday After Pentecost
	Eighteenth Sunday After Pentecost
	Nineteenth Sunday After Pentecost
Stewards	Epiphany
	Eighth Sunday After Epiphany
	Trinity Sunday
Stewardship	January 1—New Year's Day
	Trinity Sunday
	Thanksgiving Day
Still small voice	Third Sunday of Advent
	January 1—New Year's Day
	Twelfth Sunday After Pentecost
Stone rolled away	Easter Sunday
	Easter Sunday (Alternate)
Strangers	Eighth Sunday After Pentecost
Strength	Third Sunday of Advent
	Second Sunday After Epiphany
	Fourth Sunday After Epiphany
	Monday of Holy Week
	Tuesday of Holy Week
	Fourth Sunday After Pentecost
	Twenty-first Sunday After Pentecost
Struggle	Second Sunday of Easter
	Fourth Sunday After Pentecost
	Fifth Sunday After Pentecost
Suffering	First Sunday After Christmas
	Ash Wednesday
	Third Sunday of Lent
	Sixth Sunday of Lent (Passion Sunday)
	Good Friday
	Fourth Sunday of Easter
	Seventh Sunday of Easter

	Eighth Sunday After Pentecost
	Fifteenth Sunday After Pentecost
Sustenance	Second Sunday After Epiphany
	Trinity Sunday
	Thanksgiving Day
Swords and plowshares	First Sunday of Advent
Sympathy	Nineteenth Sunday After Pentecost
	Twenty-fifth Sunday After Pentecost
Taxes	Sixteenth Sunday After Pentecost
Teacher	Sixth Sunday of Lent (Palm Sunday)
	Twenty-fourth Sunday After Pentecost
Temptation	First Sunday After Christmas
	First Sunday of Lent
	Sixth Sunday of Lent (Passion Sunday)
Thirst	Third Sunday of Advent
	January 1—New Year's Day
	Seventh Sunday After Epiphany
	Third Sunday of Lent
	Sixth Sunday of Easter
	Eleventh Sunday After Pentecost
Togetherness	Christmas Day (Alternate 1)
	Eighth Sunday After Epiphany
	Third Sunday of Easter
Tongue	Sixth Sunday of Lent (Passion Sunday)
	Sixth Sunday of Lent (Palm Sunday)
Transfiguration	Last Sunday After Epiphany (Transfiguration)
Transformation	Last Sunday After Epiphany (Transfiguration)
	Sixth Sunday of Easter
	Pentecost Sunday
	Fifteenth Sunday After Pentecost
	Twenty-second Sunday After Pentecost
Treasures in heaven	Ash Wednesday
Trinity	Trinity Sunday
	Third Sunday After Pentecost
	Sixth Sunday After Pentecost
Trust	First Sunday After Christmas
	Sixth Sunday After Epiphany
	Second Sunday of Easter
	Third Sunday After Pentecost

	Nineteenth Sunday After Pentecost
	Twentieth Sunday After Pentecost
Visions	Last Sunday After Epiphany (Transfiguration)
	Third Sunday of Easter
	Ascension
	Pentecost Sunday
Wanderers	Seventh Sunday of Easter
Water	Third Sunday of Advent
	January 1—New Year's Day
	Third Sunday of Lent
	Fourth Sunday of Easter
	Fourth Sunday After Pentecost
	Eighth Sunday After Pentecost
Way, truth, life	Fifth Sunday of Easter
Waywardness	Third Sunday of Lent
	Sixteenth Sunday After Pentecost
Weakness	Third Sunday of Advent
	Fourth Sunday After Epiphany
	Fifth Sunday After Epiphany
	Fourth Sunday of Lent
	Sixth Sunday of Lent (Passion Sunday)
Wealth	Thanksgiving Day
Weariness	Fourth Sunday of Advent
	Wednesday of Holy Week
	Fifth Sunday After Pentecost
Weeds	Ninth Sunday After Pentecost
Welcome	Second Sunday of Advent
	Christmas Eve/Day
	Christmas Day (Alternate 1)
	First Sunday After Christmas
	January 1—New Year's Day
	Ash Wednesday
	Fourth Sunday of Lent
	Fifth Sunday of Lent
	Third Sunday After Pentecost
	Twelfth Sunday After Pentecost
	Thirteenth Sunday After Pentecost
	Twenty-second Sunday After Pentecost
Wholeness	Ash Wednesday
	Good Friday
	Nineteenth Sunday After Pentecost

Index of Themes and Key Words   255

Wickedness	Seventeenth Sunday After Pentecost
	Nineteenth Sunday After Pentecost
	Twenty-first Sunday After Pentecost
Wild grapes	Twentieth Sunday After Pentecost
Wind	Second Sunday of Lent
	Fifth Sunday of Lent
	Monday of Holy Week
	Pentecost Sunday
	Twenty-first Sunday After Pentecost
Wisdom	Fourth Sunday After Epiphany
	Sixth Sunday After Epiphany
	Tuesday of Holy Week
	Second Sunday After Pentecost
Witness	Epiphany
	Ash Wednesday
	Fourth Sunday of Lent
	Monday of Holy Week
	Easter Sunday
	Fifth Sunday of Easter
	Ascension
	Seventh Sunday of Easter
	Eighth Sunday After Pentecost
	Ninth Sunday After Pentecost
	Twelfth Sunday After Pentecost
Wolves	Fifth Sunday After Pentecost
Wonderful Counselor	Christmas Eve/Day
Word	Christmas Day (Alternate 2)
	First Sunday of Lent
	Fifth Sunday of Lent
	Third Sunday of Easter
	Second Sunday After Pentecost
	Seventh Sunday After Pentecost
	Eighth Sunday After Pentecost
	Thanksgiving Day
Works	Good Friday
	Fifth Sunday of Easter
	Pentecost Sunday
	Second Sunday After Pentecost
	Tenth Sunday After Pentecost
World	Eighth Sunday After Pentecost
	Fifteenth Sunday After Pentecost
Worthiness	First Sunday of Lent
	Eighteenth Sunday After Pentecost

About the Author

For the past seven years, Lavon Bayler has served on the staff of the Illinois Conference, United Church of Christ, as Area Minister in the Northern Association. For twenty years before this appointment, she served as a parish pastor. When ordained in 1959 with her husband, Robert L. Bayler, she was among the first women to achieve clergy status in the Evangelical and Reformed Church.

An alumna of the University of Northern Iowa and the Lancaster and Eden seminaries, Pastor Bayler served churches in central Ohio and in Hinckley, Barrington, and Carpentersville, Illinois. She has been active in church camping, youth work, Christian education groups, women's issues, and community concerns. Some of her previous writing has appeared in *Bread for the Journey* and *Flames of the Spirit* (The Pilgrim Press) and, earlier, in *Youth, The Messenger,* and the *Church School Worker.*

The Baylers are parents of three sons: David, a recent graduate of Kalamazoo College, who prepared the indexes for this book; Jonathan, who just completed his studies at Iowa State; and Timothy, a senior in high school. Bob is Vice-President for Religion and Health for the UCC-related Evangelical Health Systems. The family resides in Elgin, Illinois.